AWESOME BATTLES

FOR KIDS

REVOLUTIONARY WAR

BY

RYAN RHODERICK

"There is nothing so likely to produce peace as to be well prepared to meet an enemy."

—George Washington, 1780

CONTENTS

1. INTRODUCTION

Figure 1. American Revolutionary War

The American Revolutionary War is arguably one of the most important wars ever fought. It changed the world as we know it because, without the Revolutionary War, there would be no United States of America.

There have been dozens of revolutionary wars in different areas of the world. Even today, wars of revolution are being fought. We will look closely at what a revolutionary war means in the next chapter.

For the American Revolutionary War, it is essential to know that it was the first time a colony had stood up to its colonizers and won. Later, many other colonies would take their own shots at independence; some were successful, while others were not.

Britain had one of the most powerful armies in the entire world, and as we'll see in later chapters, the Continental Army stood up to them without fear. The Americans were fighting for their chance at freedom, something they cared deeply about. The soldiers from America may not have been as well-trained, equipped, or funded as the British Army, but they proved that heart is what really matters on the battlefield.

Some of the cities that saw the most action in the Revolutionary War include Boston, New York City, and Charleston. And the most famous battlefields, like Bunker Hill, are ones you can still visit today to learn even more about the battles that took place there.

The causes of the American Revolution, as we will see, are numerous. They range from taxation from the British monarchy, which led to the famous "No taxation without representation!" chants, to Great Britain imposing martial law in Massachusetts. The effects of the American Revolution are also widespread. The American Revolution inspired many other countries to stand up against their oppressors. And within America itself, the Founding Fathers created the Constitution and established one of the world's first democratic and capitalist societies.

The battles we will witness show astounding acts of bravery, tragic defeats, and bloody stalemates. From the first "unofficial" battle of the American Revolutionary War at Lexington and Concord to the final British surrender at the Battle of Yorktown and everything in between. We'll see the Continental Army carve a path to victory. But, of course, their path didn't always feel victorious.

The Americans faced defeat several times in the middle of the war, which encouraged them to seek aid from France. France was not the only international ally to get involved in the American Revolutionary War. Spain, the Netherlands, Germany, and various Native American tribes also participated in the fight. Without the aid of these countries, the war could have turned out very differently.

There are many key figures involved in the American Revolutionary War. It is vital to keep all the leaders and generals straight to fully understand who led what battle or was defeated. George Washington is likely one of the most recognizable figures of the Revolutionary War. Washington was the Commander in Chief of the Continental Army. Later, he became the first President of the United States. Washington led forces in critical battles like the Battle of Trenton and the Battle of Brooklyn.

King George III was the ruling monarch in Great Britain during the Revolutionary War. He never visited America during the war but appointed generals and commanded from across the ocean. George believed the colonies in America were rightfully his, and he was not going to let go of them, their citizens, and their resources without a fight.

Other decisive British figures in the American Revolution included senior commanders Charles Cornwallis, William Howe, Henry Clinton, and John Burgoyne. These British commanders led British troops and Loyalist militia members in many of the significant battles of the war.

The key American commanders included Major General Benjamin Lincoln, who led many of the troops in the Southern Battles, General Charles Lee who became famous for his failures rather than his victories, and Major General Benedict Arnold who led troops through many Northern Battles before going down in history as a traitor to the Patriots.

Some of the most important Patriots involved in the Revolution were not military generals. The Sons of Liberty and the Founding Fathers were both groups that had famous members like Thomas Jefferson, John Adams, Alexander Hamilton, Paul Revere, and John Hancock. Some of these men fought as soldiers in the war, some were members of the Continental Congress, and others left their stamp on American history through their organization of riots and revolts before the war. Alexander Hamilton was essential to the Continental Army's success at the Battle of Yorktown. His quick thinking allowed the Continental Troops to surprise the British troops quietly.

The Revolutionary War wasn't all about the battles, and the United States didn't magically organize itself with the snap of a finger as soon as the last gun was shot. After many battles, we will examine the after-effects of the war, including the peace treaties and how the Constitution was created. While the official years of the war range from 1775 to 1783, the causes leading up to the war and the effects after the war make this historical period nearly 20 years. That is a lot of history to unravel.

2. DEFINITION OF REVOLUTIONARY WAR AND TERMS TO KNOW

French Revolution   Spanish Revolution

Mexican War of Independence   Haitian Revolution

Figure 2. French Revolution, Spanish Revolution, Mexican War of Independence, and Haitian Revolution

Wars of revolution are fought by one country to win freedom from a controlling country. In many cases, revolutionary wars were fought after the rise of colonialism. Colonies would fight for independence from their colonizers. Today, when someone says "revolutionary war," the American War for Independence is what comes to mind most often, but any time a country fights to overthrow the government in power, it is technically a revolutionary war.

There have been other great revolutions in world history, like the French Revolution, which lasted from 1789 to 1799. The Spanish Revolution of 1936, the Mexican War for Independence of 1810–1821, and the Haitian Revolution of

1791 to 1804 (Figure 2) are also great examples of revolutionary wars that took place outside of America.

Revolutionary wars can begin for many reasons. In most cases, they require a section of the population to be unpleased with how the government is running the country. If the people can rise against the government and overthrow it, they will have the power to put their own government in place.

Since we are examining the American Revolutionary War, there are a few terms, locations, and people to be familiar with before diving into the causes and the first battles.

Before becoming the United States of America, the land where so many people live today was simply a set of Thirteen Colonies owned by Great Britain. A *colony* is land or people controlled by an overseas power. There was a whole set of wars and invasions before and after the American Revolutionary War. The Thirteen Colonies included (Figure 3):

1. Massachusets
2. Virginia
3. New York
4. Pennsylvania
5. North Carolina
6. South Carolina
7. Georgia
8. Rhode Island
9. New Hampshire
10. Delaware
11. New Jersey
12. Connecticut
13. Maryland

Figure 3. The Thirteen British North American Colonies

These colonies were the sites of most of the battles during the Revolutionary War. New York, Massachusetts, and South Carolina saw most of the fighting. At the time, the capital of the soon-to-be new country was New York City. After the British took over New York, the temporary capital was moved to Pennsylvania. They would later flee Pennsylvania for Baltimore, Maryland. At the time, the government in the colonies was called the Second Continental Congress, and they were united under the Articles of Confederation.

There were two opposing sides during the American Revolutionary War, the *Patriots* and the *Loyalists*. The Patriots were the faction of citizens in North America who wanted independence from Britain. They were ready for war! This group included George Washington, Thomas Jefferson, and Paul Revere. The Loyalists were the faction of citizens in North America who wanted to remain under the control of Britain. They did not want to go to war. These people appreciated Britain's military protection, didn't mind paying taxes to their mother country and felt a sense of connection to Britain. An estimated 20% of the colonists were Loyalists.

Once Independence was officially declared on July 4, 1776, the American colonies established their own official army. Any battles before July 4, 1776, were fought by militias and local volunteer forces. A *militia* did not have an official uniform, it didn't have standard weapons, and it wasn't paid. One militia in Massachusetts was called the "Minute Men," these militia members became infamous for being ready to fight at a minute's notice.

The first army in North America was called the Continental Army. Upon the establishment of the army, they created uniforms, manufactured weapons, and organized their enlisted troops. Anytime the Continental Army is used going forward, it refers to the American troops.

The British Army was simply referred to as the British Army, but sometimes Patriots nicknamed them the "Red Coats." This name was used because the British Army wore red coats. The British also had the help of "Hessians," or enlisted German soldiers who fought alongside the British. Germany would not become an official country for many more years after the American Revolutionary War, but the British relied on their volunteer forces to amass enough soldiers. They accepted similar volunteer recruits from Loyalists, Native Americans, and even enslaved people.

3. HISTORICAL WEAPONS

Figure 4. Weapons in the Revolutionary War

The weapons used in the late 1700s were much different than those used in modern wars. By the start of the Revolutionary War in 1775, guns, cannons, and other firepower weapons were standard. Some militaries still used bayonets or swords for their fighting, but they weren't as advantageous as the weapons that allowed troops to fight from a distance.

In the case of the Revolutionary War, some creative items were used as weapons. At the start of the war, there was no official United States Army. Instead, most of the colonies relied on local volunteer militias. They had no official uniforms and very few weapons and ammunition. In preparation for the fighting, some Patriots and local militias stole storage of British weapons that were held in America. If they didn't have guns, soldiers had to rely on farming equipment in hand-to-hand combat for the first few minor battles of the war. Axes, tomahawks, rakes, and anything that could be used for a lethal blow were relied upon by the local militias against the British soldiers.

When soldiers first enlisted in the war, they were asked to bring their own firearms and find their own bayonets. Thankfully, the Continental Army was soon organized, and they were able to distribute more sophisticated weaponry and ammunition.

Guns

The first guns were invented in the 1300s. These early weapons were not as easy to use as the guns to come later. Soldiers had to ignite flammable material that would cause bullet-like items to pop out of barrels. Some things have always been features of guns: bullets and barrels. Even the earliest gun makers knew that projectiles worked best if they were round and shot from a cylindrical barrel.

Prior to the Revolutionary War, guns were not made in the North American colonies. They received all their weapons from trade with European countries. In 1775, that changed. The Virginia State Gun Factory was one of the first weapons manufacturers in the United States. They operated throughout the Revolutionary War and created muskets, bayonets, and gunpowder for the Continental Army.

The most famous gun of the American Revolution was the musket (Figure 5). The musket had advanced by leaps and

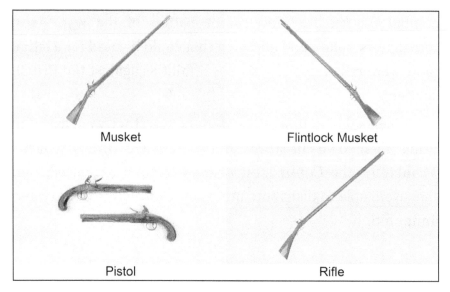

Figure 5. The Musket, Flintlock Musket, Pistol, and Rifle

bounds since the first guns in the 1300s. The musket, or flintlock musket as it was also known, was a long gun made of wood and metal. The musket was the style of gun used to shoot the first legendary shot of the Revolutionary War at the Battles of Lexington and Concord. Most of the muskets used in the Revolutionary War also had bayonets, long blades, attached to them. These guns were not as accurate as rifles.

The rifle was another popular choice during the Revolutionary War. It was more accurate than the musket but heavier and slower to load with bullets. Rifles were used for longer-range shots. The first snipers and marksmen were shooting their targets with rifles. One style of rifle, the long rifle, was the first truly American-designed gun on the market. It was created in Pennsylvania.

Pistols were occasionally used in the Revolutionary War. They had been invented by 1775, but because they were single-shot guns, they were not as effective as rifles or muskets. But pistols were easy to carry since they were only a few inches long. During a battle, a pistol would only be practical at close range. Most foot soldiers used rifles or muskets. The pistols were carried by generals and the cavalry.

Cannons

Figure 6. The Field Cannon, Mortar, Howitzer, and 24-Pound Siege Cannon

Cannons were effective weapons both on land and at sea. The different styles of cannons in 1775 included the field gun, the mortar, the howitzer, and the 24-pound siege cannon. Each of these cannons could fire different weights of cannonballs and reach different lengths. But most had a similar build. Two large wheels would support a frame that held a cylindrical barrel where the cannonballs would be shot from.

The weight of the cannon depended on the weight of the cannonball it was built to hold. For example, field guns could fire cannonballs best suited to strike enemy lines. On the other hand, the siege cannon was best suited to fire heavier cannonballs at fortifications and buildings.

The Mortar was a completely different style than the rest of the cannons. The mortar was smaller, with a thick base and a short barrel. It was best suited for aiming above enemy heads because these cannonballs would explode mid-air.

Cannons were extremely useful at sea, where cannonballs could do lots of damage to enemy ships. Soldiers developed different tactics of attack, like launching red-hot cannonballs at the enemy ships, hoping the wood would catch on fire. They also tried launching a halved cannonball tied together in the middle. This projectile could wrap itself around masts and sails to take them down.

No matter which cannon the troops used, they had to face that artillery in the 1700s was not an exact science. The field gun could fire up to 2,000 yards or as short as 1,000 yards. The soldiers with the most success behind a cannon often were the ones with the most experience. They needed time for trial and error to determine the best way to use their weapons and do the most damage.

Naval Weapons

Several battles of the Revolutionary War were fought off the coasts of port cities like Charleston, Boston, and New York.

Fighting at sea comes with an entirely different set of tactics and rules. For example, cannons are most useful at sea because they can cause large-scale damage to enemy ships. Sailors will still carry guns, but depending on the distance between the enemies, traditional guns may not have been of much use at sea.

Figure 7. The Continental Navy

The Second Continental Congress established the Continental Navy as well as the Continental Army at the same time. The Navy needed ships and experienced sailors who weren't as easy to recruit as soldiers. Eventually, the navy was supplied and ready for sea. Their first mission was to raid British ammunition storage in the Caribbean islands.

Another common tactic during naval battles included burning ships that ran aground. To stop enemy forces from taking control of a ship, the British and the Continental forces burned their defeated vessels. If they can't have it, no one can. If a ship was not burned at the end of a battle, the enemy navy would often claim that ship for their own force.

Defenses

Weapons are only as crucial as defenses. The most common defense system in the Revolutionary War was called a *Redoubt*. A redoubt is a battlefield fort that was common in North America. In Europe, permanent and large fortifications were popular at the time. The redoubts were built out of stone, wood, and earth and were meant to be easy and very quick to assemble.

The lack of training in the Continental Army meant they were unsuccessful when fighting in the standard lines that characterized the British troops. Instead, American troops won more battles when they were able to hide along treelines or behind obstacles and attack the British by surprise. A great example of this fighting technique can be seen in the Battles of Lexington and Concord. There, many Continental troops shielded themselves behind fences, barns, and high up in the trees. Knowing their troops' strengths, the Continental Army generals created hit-and-run strategies that could keep the American troops moving.

European redoubts were often minor defenses built around the central fortification, but in America, the redoubt became the main fortification. The name "redoubt" comes from the Latin term "reducere" and "reductus" which mean "refuge."

Figure 8. General Charles Lee

Another common defense during the Revolutionary War was the sizeable and permanent fort. Very few of the cities in New England had fortresses that could withstand a blow from the British Army. There was Fort George on the southern tip of Manhattan. It was armed with only a few cannons. The city did not have enough military power to man those cannons properly. In 1776, General Charles Lee (Figure 8) sought to change the landscape of permanent fortresses in America. He approached the Continental Congress with a plan for entrenchments and field fortifications all around New York City. The plan was approved, and engineers got to work on bringing Lee's vision to life.

These defenses would be crucial to the survival of American cities, and in some cases, they helped turn the tides of the war.

4. CAUSES OF THE AMERICAN REVOLUTION

Figure 9. Map of Great Britain

Before the "shot that was heard around the world," many historical events led up to the American Revolution. Some of these historical moments may sound familiar to you, but upon closer inspection, they are dramatic, tension-filled times that were essential to the start of the war.

By the time the war broke out, Great Britain (Figure 9) was basically the only major colonizing power in North America. Only the French still owned some land in Canada and to the west.

On behalf of Spain, Christopher Columbus originally sailed across the ocean in 1492. The British would not join the Spanish colonizing efforts in the Western world until 1607. In 1607, three ships reached North America from Britain, the Susan Constant, the Godspeed, and the Discovery. Aboard these ships were 100 men and boys who wanted to make their new home in America. They founded the first British colony in America, Jamestown.

Jamestown was located in modern-day Virginia. That first year in America was challenging for the colonists; many died from diseases and starvation. The water was their biggest downfall. Many settlers drank from disease-infested waters because that was all they had. But, enough remained to continue to populate North America with European settlers, a fact that the Native Americans already living there did not like.

Throughout the rest of the 1600s, Great Britain expanded their colonies in North America. Virginia had neighbors. Massachusetts, New York, the Carolinas, Connecticut, Pennsylvania, and more in the northeast were established. The original leadership style of the British monarchy toward the American colonies was very relaxed. They allowed local leadership to control most of the colony's day-to-day activities as long as they answered to the British monarchy overall. That leadership style changed in the mid-1700s.

4.1 POLITICAL AGGRESSIONS

After the Seven Years' War (1756–1763), the British government was struggling with debt. Funding a war is very expensive. So the King of Great Britain turned to the North American colonies to fix the debt issue. In his mind, half of the debt came from fighting the French in North America and protecting the colonies, so now they should pay. King George III increased the taxes paid by the colonists and increased the governmental control in the colonies but continued denying the colonists a voice in the British *Parliament*. Parliament is the ruling body that assists the king in leading the country.

One important thing to consider when reviewing these events is the amount of time that passed between each act or event. The Revolutionary War did not start overnight. Nearly ten years of aggression and political acts had to build upon one another before the Declaration of Independence would finally be drafted. It can be easy to assume that the Boston Massacre and the Boston Tea Party happened within a few weeks of one another; in reality, it was a three-year difference.

YouTube

The Seven Years War: Crash Course World History #26 by CrashCourse:

https://www.youtube.com/watch?v=joqbzNHmfWo

4.1.1 STAMP ACT
1765

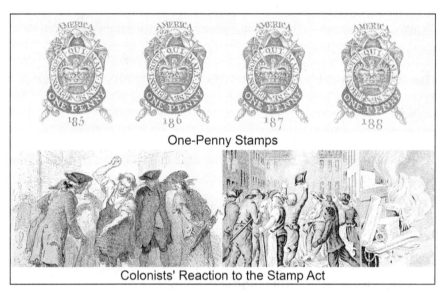

One-Penny Stamps

Colonists' Reaction to the Stamp Act

Figure 10. One-Penny Stamps and Colonists' Reaction to the Stamp Act

The Stamp Act was the first tax law passed by the British government that affected all of the colonies. Previously, each individual colony government had established what taxes the colonists would pay on their goods. The people living in the American colonies felt very little connection to Great Britain after more than 150 years of separation, yet here came the powerful country demanding money from them.

The Stamp Act imposed a tax on all paper goods sold within the colonies. This included stamps, playing cards, official documents, and paper. The full decree included more than 42 specific paper taxes and 63 clauses related to how these taxes should be collected.

The colonists were enraged. Tensions rose so high over the passing of the Stamp Act. A group of men from all the different colonies met in New York. This meeting is now known as the Stamp Congress. They discussed the colonists' position in contrast to Great Britain. It was the first unified meeting across the colonies and would pave the way for later meetings for independence.

The uproar from the colonists was intense. They rioted, refused to purchase British goods, and created other problems. As a result, Parliament was forced to repeal the Stamp Act in 1766. However, their repeal of the act was quickly followed by a declaration stating that the King of Britain and Parliament had absolute power over the colonies. Britain had no intention of being thwarted by its colonies.

YouTube

The Stamp Act by NBC News Learn:
    https://www.youtube.com/watch?v=uImdEeuLNG8

4.1.2 TOWNSHEND ACTS
1767

Figure 11. Tax on Tea

A full two years passed between the Stamp Act and the Townshend Acts. Despite the passage of time, the British government still desperately needed tax money from the colonies to keep them out of debt.

The Townshend Acts taxed many items imported to the colonies, including glass, lead, paint, paper, and tea.

Once again, the colonists were enraged over the abuse of power by the British monarchy. Benjamin Franklin proclaimed that the American colonies would simply start producing their own goods rather than buying British imports. Whether or not that was a realistic idea wasn't as important, as the British believed the colonies could not replicate the goods, especially tea. So to keep the peace, the British sent soldiers to the colonies to enforce the tax laws and subdue any violence.

The British government also saw the Townshend Acts as a way to restructure the leadership in the colonies. They planned to use part of the revenue generated by the Townshend Acts taxes to pay the salaries of newly appointed governors and local leaders who would enforce the rulings of the British government on the colonies.

In the end, 24 towns across Massachusetts and Connecticut were able to boycott imported British goods. New York and the rest of New England soon followed suit and banned the import of British goods. These boycotts were arranged thanks to the Sons of Liberty, the secret society of New England business owners. The members of the Sons of Liberty are familiar names like Samuel Adams, John Hancock, Benedict Arnold, and Patrick Henry. Many of the members would later be signatories of the Declaration of Independence. The Sons of Liberty had covert meetings, secret communications, and discreetly united the colonies. They were also well known for tarring and feathering British-appointed officials in the colonies.

Around this time was also the first use of "No taxation without representation," a phrase rumored to have been coined by the Sons of Liberty. They refused British taxes without being given a seat in the British Parliament.

4.1.3 BOSTON MASSACRE
1770

Figure 12. Boston Massacre

Several years passed, during which the taxation and boycotting continued. The presence of British soldiers in the colonies was still a source of tension. In Boston alone, there were 2,000 soldiers. They first arrived in the area in 1768 aboard 50 British warships. The British saw Boston as the center of all disobedience in the American colonies. This assumption wasn't misplaced, for most of the subversive documents encouraging colonial teamwork and fighting against the British were started in Boston.

For several months there were fights between the colonists who were loyal to the British and colonists who detested British rule. Other fights broke out between colonists and soldiers.

Some colonists even resorted to vandalizing stores that still sold British imported goods. Tensions sparked after a British officer caused the death of a young boy in early 1770.

On the evening of March 5, 1770, tensions finally reached a peak. One soldier, Private Hugh White, was guarding King Street in Boston. It was snowy and dark, but angry colonists still found the soldier in the street and began taunting him. What started as a pair of boys soon became a crowd that included Henry Knox. Knox would become a Revolutionary War hero years later. That night, Knox reportedly warned the British officer not to fire his weapon or he would die himself. After several taunts and threats, the soldier finally retaliated, regardless of Knox's warning. He struck a colonist with his bayonet. The colonists immediately fought back.

They threw rocks, snowballs, and ice at the soldier. One colonist sounded the city's alarm system by ringing the church bells, so dozens of men crowded into King Street, assuming there was a fire or other emergency. At least 50 people filled the street. When they realized what was happening, they joined in on the assault of the British private. British reinforcements were also called, and Captain Thomas Preston arrived on King Street with several British soldiers. The British soldiers called for the colonists to disperse, but the skirmish continued to escalate, and the colonists continued to throw rocks and snowballs. They also hit the soldiers with clubs until one British soldier finally had enough and fired a shot into the crowd. No command had been given by Captain Preston for the action.

It is unclear if the shot was fired by accident or if the officer had more sinister intentions. Other British soldiers followed suit. They shot into the crowd for over a minute, though Preston had still not given orders to do so. When the gunfire ceased, there were five dead colonists and six badly injured.

The governor of Massachusetts, Thomas Hutchinson, was called to the scene after the shooting. There was still a crowd in the streets. Hutchinson called into the crowd that there would be an investigation into the shooting, but he needed everyone to go home. Slowly, the crowd dispersed.

The next day, Preston and his British soldiers were arrested for their actions on King Street. In the town meeting that afternoon, the citizens and leaders of Boston requested that the British soldiers be removed from the city. This decision was made mainly for the safety of the soldiers, as town leaders feared that civilians might attack them if they remained in the city. Regardless of where the soldiers were physically stationed, the opposition to British rule only grew after this event. The Sons of Liberty were still active and encouraged the colonists to continue resisting the British soldiers that remained in Boston.

YouTube

The Boston Massacre | Road to the Revolution by Pursuit of History:
https://www.youtube.com/watch?v=BlmyzIrCKdI

4.1.4 BOSTON TEA PARTY
1773

Figure 13. Boston Tea Party

Perhaps the most infamous event that led to the Revolutionary War was the Boston Tea Party. It was the first significant riot against British rule in the country.

Before the Boston Tea Party, the taste for tea had been increasing all across the Western world for hundreds of years. Companies that shipped tea from China and India to Western Europe and America were lucrative businesses. However, tea imported to Britain was heavily taxed even before the political acts of the late 1700s. The British East India Company paid a high tax on all tea it brought into Great Britain, and that cost was transferred to the consumers.

By 1773, the British had given up all their taxes in the colonies except for the tax on tea. Tea alone created a huge revenue because about 1.2 million pounds of tea were drunk in the colonies yearly. However, the colonists were not about to give up their boycott of British goods. Rather than drink tea from the British East India Company, they smuggled Dutch tea into the country. Since the Dutch didn't tax their tea the same way the British did, even paying high prices to smuggle tea was still cheaper than the British taxed tea. Without selling tea in the colonies, the British East India Company was facing bankruptcy.

In December 1773, three British ships carrying tea from the East docked at Griffin's Wharf in Boston. These ships were legally required to unload their products within 20 days of docking, or the government would confiscate the products. The Sons of Liberty met to plan their response. They were still angry at the state of taxation without representation, and the overreach of control Britain was attempting in the colonies. The Colonists' plan meant they would refuse to pay the tea tax or even allow the tea to be unloaded from the ships. Several men were assigned to patrol the harbor and ensure the tea was not unloaded. They appealed to the governor of Massachusetts, but he wanted the tea officials to remain firm. British officials were also unwilling to compromise.

Similar tea shipping complaints arose in other cities throughout America, but the complaints in those cities only led to resignations by businessmen and government officials.

Between 30 and 100 men, the Sons of Liberty disguised themselves as Native Americans and climbed aboard three British ships. They moved quickly and quietly in the darkness, trying not to be caught. They each lifted a box of tea and began to toss them overboard. The colonists ripped open boxes and tea bags so the water would completely spoil them. At least 342 boxes of tea were dumped into the harbor. In terms of today's currency, it would be equal to roughly $1.7 million. The group continued until no tea remained on board the ships. No attempts were made to stop them.

Some of the Founding Fathers, including Washington and Jefferson, rebuked the actions of the Sons of Liberty that night. But even those who didn't support the Tea Party had to admit that it was the inciting incident for the country's Declaration of Independence. Samuel Adams wrote to defend the actions of the Boston Tea Party. He claimed it was not a riot but a group of people fighting for their rights.

In retaliation for the Boston Tea Party, King George III passed the Coercive Acts, which closed Boston Harbor, ended free elections in Massachusetts, instituted Martial Law in Massachusetts, and required colonists to take in British soldiers.

The overarching meaning of the Boston Tea Party was more than the colonists' refusal to pay British taxes. It was a signal that these people defined themselves as more American than British, despite their official, legal citizenship status.

YouTube

The story behind the Boston Tea Party - Ben Labaree by TED-Ed:

https://www.youtube.com/watch?v=1cT_ZoKGhP8

4.2 DECLARATION OF INDEPENDENCE

Figure 14. The Drafting Committee of the Declaration of Independence

Many of the colonists in the Thirteen Colonies could see that war was the only option. They wanted independence. These feelings were common after the Boston Tea Party and prevailed throughout 1774 and 1775.

In 1775, Patrick Henry famously said at the Second Virginia Convention, "Give me liberty or give me death!" In 1776, Thomas Paine published his famous "Common Sense" pamphlet, which called for independence from Great Britain.

The Patriots called for a Continental Congress in Philadelphia, Pennsylvania. More than 50 delegates attended the Congress. On June 7, 1776, Richard Henry Lee gave a speech to the Continental Congress in which he called for the colonies to declare independence from Britain.

Most of the delegates agreed with Lee, and the task of writing the document was given to Thomas Jefferson. Some other delegates, including John Adams and Benjamin Franklin, assisted Jefferson and edited the document for him.

Independence was officially voted for on July 4, 1776, at the Second Continental Congress. That is why Americans celebrate the 4th of July as Independence day. However, as you will read in later chapters, some battles of the Revolutionary War, like Lexington and Concord, took place prior to July 4, 1776.

The Declaration of Independence (Figure 15) was a document that officially declared the colonies' intentions to separate themselves from British rule. It was signed by 56 men, widely regarded as the Founding Fathers. They included John Hancock, Thomas Jefferson, Benjamin Franklin, and Samuel Adams. The document begins with "When in the course of human history, it becomes necessary for one people to dissolve the political bands which have connected them with one another." Further in its paragraphs, the declaration states that all men are entitled to "life, liberty, and the pursuit of happiness."

One of the essential things the Declaration of Independence did for America was giving it a voice to international allies. If they weren't under the thumb of Great Britain, then they were open to aid from Britain's enemies. They could also trade with other countries besides Great Britain to generate revenue and fund the war. Eventually, countries like France, the Netherlands, and Morocco all recognized American independence and began to offer aid.

Figure 15. The Declaration of Independence

At first, the British monarchy rejected the declaration, claiming it was no more than a few complaints from a few colonists. They pointed out its flaws and refused to acknowledge the colonies' independence. Even some colonists had issues with specific details of the Declaration of Independence. Nevertheless, its creation had set the Revolutionary War in motion and would not be undone. What began as a radical idea, total independence, became a reality across the Thirteen Colonies.

YouTube

Understand the Declaration of Independence in 5 Minutes by Freedomists:

https://www.youtube.com/watch?v=JeuU9s1xkVQ

What you might not know about the Declaration of Independence - Kenneth C. Davis by TED-Ed:

https://www.youtube.com/watch?v=LKJMWHCUoiw

5. EARLY BATTLES

Many of the early battles of the Revolutionary War were fought before the signing of the Declaration of Independence. For the entirety of 1775 and half of 1776, American militias fought without a formally organized army or government-supplied weapons. Militias were incredibly common in the American colonies even before the first warning signs of the Revolutionary War. Years earlier, before Britain sent its troops into the colonies, the colonists had to defend themselves. They created militias that were organized by the colony and further organized by the town. Organizing these militias was often the first order of business for a new settlement. In the nearly 300 years between Europeans arriving in the Americas and the Revolutionary War, they mostly feared attacks by native populations. They needed militias to protect them from those potential attacks. The militias participated in drills several times a year so that when trouble came calling, they'd be ready. Some militia members were store owners, lawyers, and doctors who were prepared to defend their land. They were essential to the early success of the Patriots against the British.

Despite not having the full organizational support that the Continental Army would later benefit from, the militias successfully won multiple early battles of the war. As battles and skirmishes were being fought in the New England countryside, the Founding Fathers were gathered in Philidelphia, preparing to sign the Declaration of Independence. Many such events overlapped during the Revolutionary War.

Figure 16. George Washington

In the summer of 1775, a full year before the signing of the Declaration of Independence, George Washington (Figure 16) was appointed the Commander of the Continental Army, a position he would maintain throughout the entire war. Unfortunately, because of his position, he couldn't be present to sign the Declaration.

5.1 BATTLES OF LEXINGTON AND CONCORD
APRIL 19, 1775

Figure 17. Paul Revere, William Dawes, Samuel Adams, and John Hancock

The Battles at Lexington and Concord were the first battles of the Revolutionary War. After many months of rising tensions, the British planned to march into Concord and steal a growing supply of ammunition and weapons held by the colonists. They feared a full-scale rebellion by the colonists and were right to do so.

The organization of colonists who opposed British rule, the Sons of Liberty, got word from a British informant of the British plans in Concord. Paul Revere (Figure 17) took a midnight ride through the country on April 18, 1775, to warn residents of the attack.

Revere was employed by the Boston Committee of Correspondence. In this role, he carried news from Boston to New York and Philadelphia by speeding through the colonies on horseback. That night, Dr. Joseph Warren called Revere to his office and told him of the British plans. Revere was to leave a signal in the Old North Church and ride immediately to Lexington and then on to Concord.

In the steeple of the Old North Church in Boston, the Patriots hung lanterns to signal military movements. If they saw one lantern in the steeple, the British were coming by land. If they saw two lanterns in the steeple, then the British were coming by sea.

On the night of April 18th, two lanterns were hanging in the church steeple.

Revere was joined by William Dawes. The two men took different routes to warn more people and avoid capture. Dawes rode on land through Boston Neck. Revere took a rowboat across the harbor, the shorter route. Revere then rode through Charlestown, Medford, and Arlington on the way to Lexington. According to popular history, Revere announced on the roads, "The British are Coming," but it is unlikely that this is a true account because the Sons of Liberty were attempting to keep their knowledge a secret.

Dawes and Revere met back up in Lexington, where they were greeted by Samuel Adams and John Hancock, two key revolutionary leaders. Adams and Hancock fled Lexington shortly after the arrival of Dawes and Revere. At the time, they feared being arrested by British soldiers.

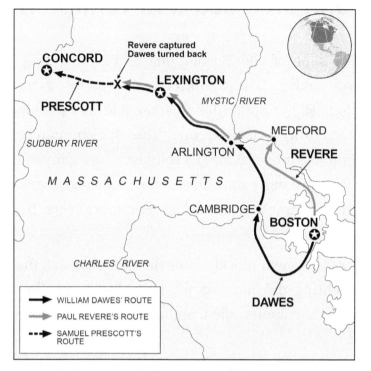

Figure 18. The routes of William Dawes, Paul Revere, and Samuel Prescott

The riders met up with a third, Samuel Prescott, who turned out to be the only rider to make it all the way to Concord. Revere was captured by the British before he could make it to Concord. They confiscated his horse but eventually allowed Revere to go free. Dawes was thrown from his horse, and he walked on foot back to Lexington.

The British troops arrived the next morning.

5.1.1 BATTLES & AFTERMATH

The first shot of the Revolutionary War was shot by an unknown soldier. The colonists had a mere 77 troops in Lexington, led by Captain John Parker, and they were met with more than 700 British troops. The British marched into Lexington just after dawn. The colonists were going to retreat in the face of danger until that anonymous shot signaled the beginning of a war that would last eight more years. It was the shot heard around the world.

Crossfire began quickly after the first shot was fired. The initial fighting did not last for long, but when the smoke cleared, eight colonists died, and only one British soldier was injured.

The British marched on toward Concord. They had minor skirmishes with Colonial militia members hiding between the towns. But, overall, they reached Concord without any major injury or disruption. When they got to Concord, they had about 220 soldiers prepared to defend the bridge into town and capture the stock of weapons. Little did they know that more than 400 Colonial militiamen were waiting up the hill.

As the British began to advance into town, Captain Issac Davis led his men toward them. Caught off guard by the large and organized Colonial militia, the British retreated to the bridge and prepared for a fight. When the British troops fired their guns, they killed Davis and Private Abner Hosmer. The Colonial militiamen fired back, killing three British soldiers and injuring several.

The British force was ordered to retreat to Boston. But first, they had 12 miles to cover between Concord and Lexington. That 12-mile trail was inundated with Colonial militiamen who attacked the British at every chance they had. The orderly retreat was turning into chaos. When the British got to Lexington on their way back to Boston, they faced the remains of Captain John Parker's forces. Parker and his troops organized a sneak attack from behind the retreating British line to avenge the death of their soldiers who had fallen earlier when the British were on their way from Boston through Lexington to Concord. Colonial militiamen shot at the British from all angles. They hid in trees, houses, and behind fences.

The British suffered heavy losses. The first battle of the Revolutionary War would go down in history as a victory for the colonies.

In the end, the British lost 73 soldiers, 174 were wounded, and several were missing. By comparison, only 49 militiamen were killed and 39 injured.

Encouraged by the success of the small militia around Lexington and Concord, more men arrived in Boston from all the colonies. They numbered at least 20,000.

The British realized the strength of the enemy they were facing. Word of the defeat quickly spread to Britain, and the King began to arrange for more troops to be sent to America.

5.2 BATTLE OF BUNKER HILL
JUNE 17, 1775

Figure 19. Colonel William Prescott and Major General William Howe

The Battle of Bunker Hill is the second battle of the Revolutionary War. It was actually fought on Breed's Hill, but the troops believed they were on Bunker hill, so the name has remained. It is one of many battles in the Siege of Boston. British troops were scheming to besiege the city of Boston when Colonial forces got wind of their secret plans. The British hoped to occupy the land surrounding the city and later move into the city itself. The hills were vital because they would secure Boston Harbor for the British.

In response, the Colonial troops, led by Colonel William Prescott (Figure 19), marched to Breed's Hill on June 16, 1775, to defend their city. There were more than 1,000 Colonial troops present. They traveled from the nearby colonies of Vermont, New Hampshire, and Connecticut to help protect the land around Boston.

While the Colonial troops waited for the British to respond to their presence, they built defensive walls out of the earth and assembled fences to fend off attacks from the right and left. By morning, an entire redoubt was completed. The structure was six feet tall, and the trenches around it were more than 100 feet long. It was a far more organized force than the British were expecting.

The British forces numbered more than 2,200 and were led by Major General William Howe (Figure 19). They planned to attack the colonial position on Breed's hill from multiple sides. The force under Howe would attack directly from the front, and another would attack them from behind.

5.2.1 BATTLE & AFTERMATH

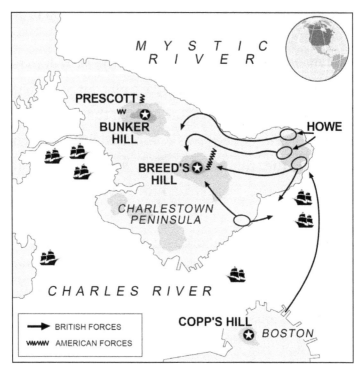

Figure 20. Locations of Breed's and Bunker Hills

"Don't fire until you see the whites of their eyes," said Colonel Prescott, allegedly, to his men when facing the British troops at the Battle of Bunker Hill. The Colonial forces lacked ammunition, and Prescott didn't want them to waste shots on far-away targets. Prescott had requested reinforcements, but few came, and those who did were difficult to lead.

The British marched closer and closer against the hidden Colonial Army. Colonial snipers who were positioned on the outskirts of Charlestown were picking off British troops one by one at a distance. Howe ordered most of the men to continue but dispatched a few soldiers to burn parts of Charlestown.

The billowing smoke of the city on fire was the backdrop to the rest of the battle. When they were a few dozen yards away, the first shot was fired from behind the colonial front lines. The Colonial Army unloaded a wall of gunfire on the British line. They had the advantage of using the fence line to steady their guns and could use the same fence for defense. The British were struggling to move forward between the heavy gunfire from the colonial front lines, the snipers, and the blaze of the town. They were forced to retreat to avoid heavy casualties.

While the British retreated, the colonists reloaded. They had used a significant amount of their ammunition but had enough left to attack from a distance again. The British reformed their fighting lines. Not only did they have to worry about colonial artillery, but they were slowed down by waist-high grass that disguised uneven ground on the hill. As they neared the redoubt at the top of Breed's Hill, they were once again met with a wall of gunfire that forced them to retreat a second time.

Prescott attempted to order the men who had remained on Bunker Hill to march forward to Breed's Hill, but not all of them followed orders. Those who were on Breed's Hill, about 700 troops with 150 actually in the redoubt, were running out of ammunition quickly. They would have little time to reorganize as the British prepared for another attack. On their third march up Bunker Hill, through grass and piles of bodies, the British made contact with the colonists and began to fight in hand-to-hand combat. The close-range fighting was brutal. Many of the colonists did not have bayonets or weapons that could cause harm at close range, so the British had the advantage. The outnumbered colonists were mostly out of ammunition, so they were forced to give up their position.

In the end, more than 200 British soldiers were killed in the Battle of Bunker Hill, but only 100 colonists died. A surprising number of British casualties were enlisted officers. There were several hundred injured or taken prisoner on both sides. The greatest loss to the Patriots was five of the six cannons they had positioned on the redoubt. Even though Bunker Hill was technically a victory for the British, the heavy losses proved that the Colonial Army would put up a strong fight.

Shortly after the Battle of Bunker Hill, on June 19, 1775, George Washington was appointed to lead the Continental Army. One of Washington's first tasks was to organize the troops and instill discipline in the mostly volunteer militia.

Despite Washington's arrival, the British held the Charlestown Peninsula. They realized the colonists were not going down without a fight.

YouTube

Battle of Bunker Hill (The American Revolution) by Simple History:

https://www.youtube.com/watch?v=9UqJzKX03-0

5.3 BATTLE OF GREAT BRIDGE
DECEMBER 9, 1775

Figure 21. Governor John Murray

John Murray, the Governor of Virginia, was wary of Patriot militias who could attack a stock of gunpowder and weapons in Williamsburg, Virginia. After the battles of Lexington, Concord, and Bunker Hill, Murray knew they could be coming for these resources next. So in an attempt to ward off any fighting, Murray instituted martial law in Virginia. The same proclamations had been made earlier that year in Massachusetts to give the military the authority to control civilians directly.

While Virginia was locked down, Murray secretly ordered British marines and Loyalist fighters to remove the weapons and gunpowder stored in Williamsburg.

Word spread throughout Virginia of Murray's plans, so hundreds of militiamen organized and headed for Williamsburg. In a panic, Murray ordered his troops to Norfolk. Norfolk was traditionally an epicenter for Loyalists, where Murray knew they would find little local retaliation. However, they needed a plan to hold off the Patriot militias. For extra support, Murray created an extra regiment of enslaved people. He promised them freedom in exchange for their service to the British Army. The British marines, combined with the "*Ethiopian Regiment*," numbered more than 400 soldiers. The Ethiopian Regiment was a military unit composed of formerly enslaved people who had escaped from their Patriot enslavers. On the other hand, the Patriot militias' numbers continued to grow, and by the time the battle was near, they had more than 800 soldiers.

At the time, there was only one way in and out of Norfolk, Virginia, the Great Bridge. It connected Virginia and North Carolina. On either side of the bridge was the Elizabeth River, a swampy, boggy area. To prepare for battle, Murray's troops built a fort on the north side of the bridge. They also removed the bridge's planks, making crossing it impossible. Then, they awaited the arrival of the Patriot militias.

5.3.1 BATTLE & AFTERMATH

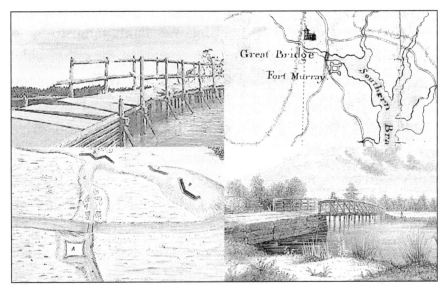

Figure 22. Great Bridge

The Patriot militia arrived on December 7, 1775, on the south side of the bridge. Fort Murray stared them down. They were led by Colonel William Woodford. Woodford was initially wary of attacking the British because he wasn't sure his men had enough firepower to defeat the well-armed garrison. To improve their chances of success, Woodford waited for additional militiamen to join his position.

Woodford and the Patriots had a few cannons that they could use to attack the British from across the river. Unfortunately, they were useless as they lacked mounts. John Murray, however, did not know the Patriot cannons were unusable. He feared a strong attack from the Patriots, so he organized to launch the first attack. Under cover of darkness, Murray's troops removed the bridge planking.

When the sun rose, the horn for battle was blown, and the British and American troops battled in the swamp and on the bridge for two days. The fighting was light, hand-to-hand combat that didn't result in many casualties for either side. Fighting in swamp waters in December proved difficult and too cold. After two days of these minor fights, Murray realized he would need to put his troops on the offensive and drive Woodford and the Patriots away from the bridge.

The British soldiers engineered an impressive strategy of firing by platoons. As one line of soldiers fired their guns, the next would have a chance to reload. They repeated this pattern as they assaulted the unsuspecting militia on the south side of the bridge.

"The day is our own!" Captain Charles Fordyce, a British commanding officer, yelled into the battlefield, and the British soldiers broke their shooting pattern to charge forward with their bayonets. The Patriot militia organized quickly, deflected shots from the British, and fired when the British got closer. British commanding officers, Fordyce and Captain Samuel Leslie, were wounded under the Patriots' gunfire. Fordyce sustained 14 shots before dying. Soon, the bridge was littered with bodies.

Woodford ordered some of his men to march off to the left. Further from the bridge and the action. The riflemen could take careful aim at the British position and fire at the side of their line. The tactic proved effective not only because they could take down many British soldiers but because they were out of the line of British fire. Because of this placement, the British could do nothing to retaliate.

Realizing the intensity of the Patriots' power, many British and Loyalist troops turned back. They retreated to their fort on the north side of the bridge.

Within a few days of the battle at Great Bridge, the Patriots moved into Norfolk. Over 100 British and Loyalist troops were killed or wounded in the battle, but only one Patriot was killed.

The Battle of Great Bridge continued to prove to the British that the Americans were a force to be reckoned with. They would not be defeated easily. After the Patriots entered Norfolk, Murray fled Virginia.

YouTube

Battle of Great Bridge by Discerning History:
    https://www.youtube.com/watch?v=xpmOQTbrI3U

The Battle of Great Bridge: A "Miniature Bunker Hill" by American Battlefield Trust:
    https://www.youtube.com/watch?v=kXfHt76ETpw

5.4 BATTLE OF QUEBEC
DECEMBER 31, 1775

Figure 23. Location of Quebec City and Montreal

The British occupied Quebec at the beginning of the Revolutionary War. Quebec, one of Canada's major cities, was an important stronghold for the British. Two American military leaders, Colonel Benedict Arnold and Major General Richard Montgomery (Figure 24), believed that if they could take control of Quebec, they could gain favor from the Canadians toward the Patriot's cause. In the original plan, General Phillip Schuyler would invade Canada alongside Arnold, but illness caused him to send Montgomery instead.

Major General Richard Montgomery   General Guy Carleton

Figure 24. Generals Richard Montgomery and Guy Carleton

The Continental Army (the army of the Thirteen Colonies), commanded by Arnold and Montgomery, began their march in the fall of 1775. Montgomery marched his troops north from Lake Champlain and captured Montreal. Arnold and his troops marched to Quebec City. After their arrival at Quebec City, they waited for Montgomery outside the city limits. While they waited, freezing temperatures made digging trenches in the icy ground impossible.

The Governor of the Province of Quebec, General Guy Carleton (Figure 24), heard of the battle at Montreal and guessed that the Continental Army was headed for Quebec City next. Carleton ordered extra fortifications to be arranged around the city.

The Patriots requested multiple times that the city surrenders without violence. However, Governor Carleton refused their order to surrender.

5.4.1 BATTLE

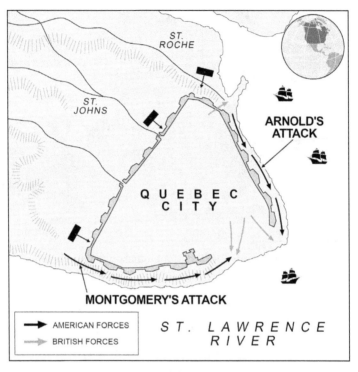

Figure 25. Map of the Battle of Quebec

Arnold and Montgomery split the Continental Army in half to attack from two sides. They had a total of 1,200 soldiers at their command, but they were outnumbered by the British force of 1,800. The two commanders planned to signal to one another when the fight began by shooting rocks into the air. Montgomery marched toward the city early in the morning of December 31, 1775. As they prepared to attack, blizzard-like conditions set in. The rock signals were not launched.

The British soldiers stationed around the city's fortresses saw Montgomery and his men coming from a mile away. Montgomery had hoped that fewer defenses would face the St.

Figure 26. Death of Montgomery

Lawrence River. The American forces made it right up to the first wall, where they hoped to infiltrate the city's defenses. But as the Patriots came closer, the British fired into their lines.

Despite the whiteout conditions, British soldiers could spot the Patriots because of the lanterns they had lit to guide them through the snow. In addition, they were armed with muskets and other heavy weaponry that caused heavy casualties to Montgomery's men, including Montgomery himself, who was killed instantly (Figure 26). Without a commander to lead them forward, the forces retreated.

At the same time, Arnold led his half of the troops toward Quebec from the north. The British were ready on this side, too. They had a battery of guns and cannons that shot into the American troops. Because of the high walls surrounding Quebec, it was difficult for the American forces to shoot back accurately.

Despite difficulties, the troops made more progress in the north than in the south. They fought their way over the first wall and were supposed to meet Montgomery's men at a pre-planned meeting point. Unfortunately, they didn't know that the attack in the city's south had retreated. There were no reinforcements.

The Continental Army attempted to fight the British troops they encountered inside the city, but their guns began to run out of ammunition or break due to the weather. American commanders finally called off the attack because the blizzard conditions were too intense. The British troops were organizing within the city, and the defeat of the American forces was inevitable. Here too, the Americans suffered heavy casualties. Arnold was shot in the leg.

YouTube

Battle of Quebec | Animated History by The Armchair Historian:

https://www.youtube.com/watch?v=aS2tJBi13bI

5.4.2 AFTERMATH

After this initial attack, Colonel Benedict Arnold tried to besiege Quebec City again, but Governor Carleton had stored enough provisions to wait out the freezing winter.

More than 400 of the Continental Army's original 1,200 soldiers were killed, captured, or wounded in the Battle of Quebec. The Americans failed to take the city and left the area entirely by early spring.

The Continental Army halted any further plans to invade Canada after this defeat. Not only did the Battle of Quebec fail to persuade French Canadians to help the American cause, but it cost them many lives.

Years later, the same Benedict Arnold, who showed incredible bravery in the Battle of Quebec, would become a traitor to the Continental Army. He was given a command position in the British Army and a large sum of cash in exchange for giving up the American position at the Hudson River. The whole arrangement was uncovered when the Continental Army captured a British spy carrying papers and letters about the plan.

YouTube

Benedict Arnold: America's Greatest Traitor by Biographics:
https://www.youtube.com/watch?v=PEcd7eOnLIU

5.5 BATTLE OF BROOKLYN
AUGUST 26, 1776

Figure 27. Map of New York City

New York was a crucial state throughout the entire war. It was an epicenter for life in the colonies, a massive port city, and a strategic location for easily moving into other parts of the Northeast.

In 1776, New York City did not look anything like the city you might imagine today. It was a primarily rural area; imagine that! The urbanized area was filled with mostly three to four-story buildings, wide dirt roads, and the harbor. The area of Long Island we now call Brooklyn was mostly fields. Some buildings from this time still exist in 21st-century New York City, like the St. Paul Church, which is now nestled into the manufacturing zone of the city. Back in the years of the war, the church was occupied as a hospital for soldiers.

Just like the Americans, the British knew that holding New York City would give them an incredible advantage. The Patriots began the complex process of building defenses around New York City, but the work was slow, and they lacked enough workers to do a good job. General Charles Lee pointed out that all the defenses in the world would not save New York if the British were attacking from the sea. Despite these difficulties, they successfully built several redoubts throughout the city and constructed Fort Stirling across the river, facing the city. Three other forts near Fort Stirling were under construction at the time, and they had a line of 36 cannons between them. Lee also removed all known Loyalists from New York so the British wouldn't have any help from the inside. Previously, the British had stationed themselves in Boston, but they found the position too challenging. They left the city in March 1776 and boarded ships to await reinforcements. During their escape from Boston, the British set their sights on New York.

On August 22, 1776, 10,000 extra British soldiers docked at Gravesend Bay in Long Island. They came on more than 130 ships. Their arrival made the combined British forces about 20,000 strong. The Americans were outnumbered, as George Washington led a force of only 10,000. Those troops that Washington did have were still untrained, some lacked weapons, and infighting was becoming a substantial problem.

Figure 28. The Continental Army

The Continental Army was split between Manhattan and Brooklyn with no way of reinforcing one another. George Washington felt confident that he wouldn't be able to beat the British forces, but he hoped he could cause heavy casualties and hold them off for a while.

Even though the war truly began with the Battles of Lexington and Concord, the Battle of Brooklyn was the first fight after the Declaration of Independence was signed. It was also the largest battle of the entire war, engaging the most number of troops on either side. The whole continent held its breath to see the outcome of the first official battle since America had laid out its intentions.

5.5.1 BATTLE

Figure 29. Map of the Battle of Brooklyn

In the weeks before the official start of the battle, British ships antagonized the city. Two ships, the Phoenix and the Rose, sailed toward the Hudson River. Continental Army cannons were fired at the ships from the forts, but it did not deter the ships from shooting their cannon artillery into the city. The true goal of these British ships was to block the American supply lines coming in and out of the city. Despite the cannon fire, the British were able to sail through the Hudson River.

Major General William Howe (Figure 19) of the British Army gave General Washington (Figure 16) of the Continental Army one chance at surrendering the city without a fight. He

Figure 30. Henry Knox and Samuel Webb

sent a messenger with a letter for Washington in mid-July. Washington sent Henry Knox and Samuel Webb (Figure 30) to intercept the messenger on his behalf. He refused to acknowledge the first letter because it was addressed simply to "George Washington" and did not address his rank as "General" of the Continental Army. Washington knew that not only himself but the young country of America needed the recognition of independence and importance from the British General. He continued to ignore or deny any letters that were not appropriately addressed.

After many failed negotiations, the actual battle began on August 27, 1776. The British soldiers attacked the Continental forces in the south at Guan Heights. As the 20,000 British came ashore from their docked naval vessels, they were met with a mere 500 Continental soldiers armed with rifles. The gunfire began almost immediately.

At first, the Continental soldiers successfully picked off British troops from afar. As the British moved out from their ships toward Guan Heights, Washington hoped the Americans would have the advantage. Guan Heights was a series of hills more than 100 feet tall. Most of the Continental troops waited atop the hills. An elevated position, Washington hoped, would allow them to inflict heavy casualties before falling back to Brooklyn Heights. Despite their defensive position on the hills, the British soon gained the advantage by finding a hole in the American defenses. Jamaica Pass, a road to the east of the American frontlines, was virtually unguarded because Washington did not order the troops to spread out enough. The British were able to fight past the five patrolling officers at Jamaica Pass and sneak 10,000 troops and 14 cannons through the road to attack the Continental Army from multiple sides. The rest of the Continental Army was unaware they had been breached as the march took place at night and the fight on the frontlines was still underway.

By morning, the American forces were nearly surrounded. The fighting came to a head on a hill in Kings County, now known as "Battle Hill." There, the Continental soldiers were able to inflict the most damage in the entire battle. It was close, brutal fighting with bayonets. Though the British had an advantageous position on the hill, they were not expecting such a strong American presence after the ease of marching through Jamaica Pass. At first, excited by their success, the Americans did not realize that the British troops on Battle Hill were not the main coalition of British forces. When word finally reached them that thousands more soldiers had been spotted, the

Figure 31. Major General William Alexander

Continental Army began to pull back to their reinforcements to Brooklyn Heights in the north.

One contingent of soldiers, known as the Maryland 400, did not flee with the rest of their comrades. They were led by Major General William Alexander. These brave soldiers who made up the Continental rearguard led an offensive attack on more than 2,000 British soldiers in order to give their fellow men more time to escape. The Maryland 400 attacked, fell back, and attacked again. They repeated this cycle until there were not enough men to fight. More than 250 of them died in close quarters fighting the British, but their actions allowed most of the remaining Continental Army to escape. Less than 12 of the Maryland 400 would make it back to the American lines. The remaining survivors were taken prisoners by the British.

General Charles Cornwallis   General William Heath

Figure 32. General Charles Cornwallis and General William Heath

It is rumored that George Washington witnessed the attack from a redoubt across the river and praised the fallen soldiers for their bravery. In the days after the fighting, General Charles Cornwallis of Britain said that Major General William Alexander and the Maryland 400 "fought like wolves."

The full power of the Continental Army was trapped in Brooklyn Heights, the East River was behind them, and the full force of the British Army was before them. General William Howe began preparations for a renewed attack on Washington and his troops the next morning. The true motive behind Howe's plan for an organized siege is unknown. Many believe he wanted to avoid heavy British casualties and others say he was giving Washington a chance to surrender. Meanwhile, Washington had no intentions of being attacked, slaughtered, imprisoned, or surrendered. He knew that his stand had come to an end.

Washington sent a messenger to General William Heath (Figure 32) in the Bronx. The messenger carried instructions to Heath to send Washington and the troops as many boats as possible. As the ships began to arrive, Washington sent fake orders for the troops to gather for a night attack. Instead, they were ordered into silence and quieted even the wagon wheels. Under cover of darkness, Washington then ordered his troops across the East River and into New Jersey. The remaining Continental Army, roughly 9,000 soldiers, was able to move across the river without arousing suspicion from the British troops. They were helped by a fog that fell over the city. Not a single soldier perished in the retreat.

In the morning, Howe marched toward the Continental Army's position from the night before, only to find the entire army had disappeared.

YouTube

The Battle of Brooklyn (Long Island): The Revolutionary War in Four Minutes by American Battlefield Trust:

https://www.youtube.com/watch?v=aLdwqoXxOtI

5.5.2 AFTERMATH

Figure 33. Battle of Brooklyn

The Battle of Brooklyn was a victory for the British. They only lost 388 of their 20,000 soldiers to death, injuries, or capture. The British would retain control of New York City for the remainder of the war.

The Continental Army had suffered heavy casualties. They lost more than 2,000 troops to death, injury, or capture. None of those losses were sustained during the retreat. That nighttime retreat has been regarded by some military historians as one of the greatest military feats of all time. Still, the defeat was a heavy blow to the morale of the Continental Army, which had been quite successful up until the Battle of Brooklyn. Many of their imprisoned soldiers would spend the rest of the war trapped in New York City, either aboard British ships just off the harbor or in Fort Greene in Brooklyn.

The following battles would be largely centered around New York as the Continental Army attempted to retake the city. They would eventually evacuate to New Jersey and later to Pennsylvania.

In the years after the war, the new American government made strengthening the forts around New York Harbor one of their top priorities. They could never allow one of their most important cities to be so exposed again.

5.6 BATTLE OF TRENTON
DECEMBER 26, 1776

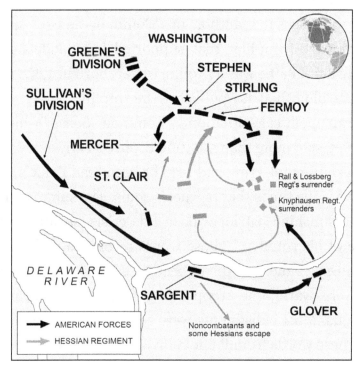

Figure 34. Map of the Battle of Trenton

The Patriots were not as confident coming into the Battle of Trenton. They had suffered heavy losses, lacked funding, and their enlistments were slowing. Moreover, George Washington wasn't sure where to turn next after he fled across the Delaware River to Pennsylvania and set up camp. The British forces were in better spirits, having won two previous battles, but they were not expecting the Battle of Trenton. Only 1,400 men were stationed in Trenton, and none of them believed the Continental Army would attack in the dead of winter.

At the Patriots' camp, Washington ordered the men read Thomas Paine's "The American Crisis," a pamphlet meant to invigorate and support the colonists' goal of independence. Paine was also the author of "Common Sense," another revolutionary pamphlet that supported independence from Great Britain. Paine was a prolific writer; born in 1737, he was 39 years old when he published his prolific essays on the American political situation. "Common Sense," his first pamphlet, sold more than 500,000 copies. Nearly every soldier in the Continental Army had read or been read Paine's words. "These are the times that try men's souls. The summer soldier and the sunshine patriot will, in this crisis, shrink from the service of his country." Those words resonated with the cold and hungry soldiers who had been so eager to fight when the days were warm, the troops were fed, and the army was victorious. Most enlistments were set to expire on January 1, 1777. These words from Paine reinvigorated the soldiers.

Sensing a change in mood, Washington decided to attack the British once more, surprise them, and potentially shift the attitude of the remaining Colonial soldiers.

5.6.1 BATTLE

Figure 35. Battle of Trenton

On Christmas day, December 25, 1776, George Washington put his plan into action. If all went according to plan, one group of soldiers would attack just north of Trenton to stop aid from reaching the British soldiers stationed there. One group would block the bridge, the only escape route for the British soldiers in Trenton. Washington himself would lead more than 2,000 soldiers directly into Trenton to attack the garrison. With a plan in place, the forces that camped with Washington along the Delaware River, roughly 6,200 soldiers, boarded boats and took the perilous journey back across the icy water. Unfortunately, due to the weather, the first two battalions of soldiers could not get across the river. Only Washington's self-directed group of 2,000 remained. They marched ten miles to Trenton, New Jersey.

Figure 36. Colonel Johann Rall

Right outside of Trenton, Washington separated the forces into two groups. They were going to attack from two sides, north and west.

For several weeks, smaller coalitions of militiamen had been attacking the garrison in Trenton. German Colonel Johann Rall, commander of the *Hessian troops*, had used up nearly all his energy and supplies to protect the stash of British resources held there. As the sun rose on December 26, 1776, Rall was not expecting the Colonial troops. The surprise attack was off to a successful start.

The Continental Army, led by Washington, first attacked an outpost at River Road manned by *Hessian troops*. The Hessians were 30,000 German troops hired by the British to help fight during the Revolutionary War. At first, the Hessians believed the attack to be another small group of militiamen, but soon they realized there were more troops present than a simple raiding militia. The American forces outgunned the Hessians and forced them out of the outpost, exposing a route into Trenton. As they retreated back towards the main town of Trenton and their British reinforcements, Washington ordered a section of his troops to march through the exposed route at River Road. He then directed another section of soldiers to block any escape routes to Princeton, New Jersey that the British could try to use.

One section of Washington's army rained down gunfire on the area around the garrison. The other section fought in hand-to-hand combat with the British troops directly in the garrison. The unsuspecting British Army was falling fast. They began to retreat. In the chaos, Colonel Johann Rall was shot. Without a leader, the British troops ran, but many were captured. Finally, the Americans seized the British garrison, which was full of guns and ammunition. It was an apparent American victory.

YouTube

Trenton | Battles of America by FreedomProject Media:
   https://www.youtube.com/watch?v=B0x3Vln34AQ

Washington's Crossing of the Delaware River: The Revolutionary War in Four Minutes by American Battlefield Trust:
   https://www.youtube.com/watch?v=6M5sYsiVG_Q

5.6.2 AFTERMATH

Figure 37. George Washington crossing the Delaware River

All in all, zero Continental soldiers were killed in the Battle of Trenton. Washington's men took at least 900 prisoners from the British Army. Twenty British soldiers were dead, and 80 more were wounded. Rall died soon after the fighting ceased, but not before surrendering to George Washington.

The famous painting of George Washington crossing the Delaware River was created as a result of this famous American victory over the British. In the piece, Washington stands bravely against the chill and the darkness as he guides his men across the icy Delaware River (Figure 37). It is possibly one of the most famous paintings of the entire Revolutionary War.

The fifth President of the United States, James Monroe, was a lieutenant in the Battle of Trenton. Long before he became president in 1817, he was an 18-year-old fighter who was shot in battle. Upon his recovery, Monroe was promoted to captain.

Washington and the Continental Army returned to Pennsylvania after their success in Trenton, and they would secure another victory a few weeks later in Princeton, New Jersey.

5.7 BATTLES OF SARATOGA
SEPTEMBER 19 & OCTOBER 7, 1777

General John Burgoyne · General Horatio Gates

Figure 38. Generals John Burgoyne and Horatio Gates

Two years into the Revolutionary War, the British had failed to secure Charleston, South Carolina, they had fled their position in Boston but had successfully occupied New York City. They sensed that the New England colonies were home to more Patriots than Loyalists, so they formulated a plan to isolate the Patriots. If successful, the British war efforts in this area would cut off New England from the rest of the colonies.

Their strategy involved attacking the local militia from three sides, hoping to have the separate armies meet in Albany, New York. British General John Burgoyne (Figure 38) was the leader of this movement. The original British plan called for three separate units to converge from the north, west, and

Figure 39. Location of Saratoga

south near Albany, New York. The northern coalition would march south from Montreal. The western group would march east from Ontario. The Southern troops would march north from New York City.

Despite their best hopes, the British plan was falling apart. The southern coalition had disregarded the plan and instead marched west to begin the Philadelphia Campaign. The western coalition was stopped at a fort. They fought the Continental soldiers and could not advance. So, Burgoyne and the forces from the north were all alone. He had even lost some of his allied Indian support after their loss at the Battle of Bennington a few weeks earlier.

Winter was approaching, so Burgoyne needed to establish a camp. He had two options, turn back toward Montreal or continue to Albany. Burgoyne chose to advance to Albany with his 6,000 troops.

On the American side, a force of 8,500 was led by General Horatio Gates (Figure 38). Gates had newly inherited his command from General Philip Schuyler. His innovative skills impressed George Washington, who sent Gates additional troops and some of his best commanders, like Benedict Arnold, to help with the northern front. The Patriots knew that they could not allow the British to separate all of New England from the rest of the country and they were prepared to fight to the death to stop Burgoyne.

Unfortunately, Burgoyne of the northern coalition was met by the Continental Army 15 miles away from Albany. He lacked the aid from the other sections of the British Army that he had counted on. He had defeated several smaller Continental coalitions, occupied forts, and moved throughout upstate New York until he came to Saratoga.

5.7.1 BATTLES

Figure 40. Map of the Battles of Saratoga

Gates and his men erected a large wall in the bluffs above the Hudson River. This wall was nearly a mile long and hid 22 cannons behind it. The Continental Army also built smaller, trench-like defenses in the bluffs so they could see the river and the road simultaneously. The only road to Albany passed directly by their position.

While they awaited the arrival of the British forces, tensions began to rise in the camp and surrounding areas. A few American scouts that Gates had sent to spy on the British position had fallen into a brief skirmish with British soldiers.

After a brief trip to Fort Stanwix, General Benedict Arnold egged on soldiers who preferred General Schulyer to Gates. Eventually, the tensions between Gates and Arnold would result in Arnold's request for a transfer, leaving the forces at Saratoga. Thankfully, news of the British nearing the Continental Army's position deflated the tensions at camp. The Continental Army readied itself for battle.

With roughly 6,000 troops, the British were forced to come by road since heavy tree lines restricted their movement. When they arrived in September of 1777, they were outnumbered.

Burgoyne divided his troops into three separate columns. Gates divided his troops similarly, giving special attention to the left flank. That column of soldiers advanced toward the British group at Freeman's Farm. In their advanced position, the Americans could rely on their strongest skill, fighting while hidden in a tree line. Gunfire was exchanged between the two sides as the British marched closer. They were slightly delayed because of obstacles the American troops had placed on the road. The two sides battled for hours. General Daniel Morgan (Figure 41) placed marksmen, skilled shooters, at key points on the battlefield. They were able to aim and fire at most British officers marching toward them. The battle continued in waves of intense artillery fire and lulls as both sides repaired damages and reinforced their troops. The sun went down before they could declare a victor. The British needed reinforcements, and despite an extra 500 troops, they lost ground and at least 600 of their own men. The Continental Army was resupplied faster. They had at least 13,000 troops among them.

Figure 41. General Daniel Morgan

In an attempt to defeat the Continental Army before their resources ran out, the British sent a force to the American position in the bluffs above the river. They were hoping for an element of surprise, but the Patriots caught word of the British plan. They were ready with a strong defense. Riflemen from behind the American line of defense rained down a continual pour of gunfire. Because the American position was high up on a bluff, the British did not have a proper angle to return fire. When the British attempted to charge the defenses with a group of bayonet-wielding soldiers, the Americans finally charged forward from their defensive position and fought with the British at close range. One of the British Majors was shot in battle. The fighting pushed the British all the way back to their base. But the Americans did not stop at that; they continued to fight. The base was not strong enough to withstand the Continental Army.

The Continental Army's sharpshooters were still stationed in their key spots during the second battle round. Their strong aim almost killed General Burgoyne. His horse, hat, and waistcoat were shot, but he managed to escape the battlefield alive.

On October 8, 1777, the British attempted to escape from their camp but were stopped closer to Saratoga. The remaining troops were out of supplies, hungry and weak. It was easy for the American soldiers to surround the British and continue inflicting heavy casualties. Finally, on October 17th, British General Burgoyne surrendered (Figure 42).

YouTube

Battle of Saratoga (American Revolution) by History Heroes:
  https://www.youtube.com/watch?v=BXQRf2QBegk

Battle of Saratoga: A Turning Point in the Revolutionary War by Daily Dose Documentary:
  https://www.youtube.com/watch?v=jFEtLT4_5D4

5.7.2 AFTERMATH

Figure 42. Surrender of General Burgoyne

An estimated 440 British soldiers were killed in the Battles of Saratoga; a surprising number of them were officers. Only 90 American soldiers were killed. The British also suffered worse injury rates than the Continental Army.

The French monarchy was impressed with the Continental Army's ability to defend against the British Army, which was highly regarded as the most impressive in the world at the time. As a result, the French were prepared to send resources like guns and ammunition to the colonies. Shortly after the promise of French support, the Spanish and the Dutch made similar contributions to the American cause.

Similar to other American victories, the success at the Battles of Saratoga lifted the spirits of the Patriots. True victory over the British seemed possible.

Figure 43. George Washington makes his headquarters at West Point

But not all was well in the wake of the Battles of Saratoga. General Benedict Arnold was honored after the battle with a position at West Point. He also suffered a leg wound that left him bedridden while he recovered. During his recovery, Arnold began communications with the British that would turn him into a traitor against the Continental Army. The plan was for Arnold to take command at West Point and then turn the fort over to the British.

YouTube

The History of West Point by West Point Admissions:
https://www.youtube.com/watch?v=htMOe7t5ioA

6. MID-WAR BATTLES

Figure 44. Mid-War Battles

By 1778, the tides of the war had changed several times. The Continental Army saw early success at the Battles of Lexington and Concord and Bunker Hill, but as the war continued, the more experienced British Army began to defeat the Patriots. The British were more adept at traditional European fighting styles that involved formal organizations of troops in fields. The American troops were still mostly untrained even three years into the war, so they did not succeed in these traditional battles. Sneak attacks and guerrilla warfare suited the American troops better.

The first goal of the British was to focus on the Northern Campaign. They fled Boston to successfully take New York City in the early years of the war. But, after three years of battles, the British Army was focused on the Philadelphia Campaign.

The British success in New York City had forced American troops out of the area. They wanted to take a stronghold of Pennsylvania because the Americans had moved the Congress to Philadelphia. Amidst the fighting in the mid-war battles, the Americans were forced to move the Capitol once again. In 1780, the British set their sights on a new area of the country and aimed for success in the Southern Colonies.

Many of the battles in this time period are regarded as ties. They include Barren Hil, Monmouth, Rhode Island, and Savannah. The key figures in these battles are many of the same faces from the first years, like George Washington and Charles Cornwallis. However, Charles Lee of the Continental Army becomes an essential character in the story of American independence around this time.

6.1 BATTLE OF MONMOUTH
JUNE 28, 1778

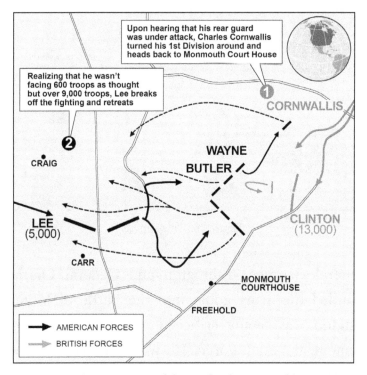

Figure 45. Map of the Battle of Monmouth

The Battle of Monmouth was one of the first major battles after the Continental Army's winter training camp at Valley Forge (Figure 46). Washington described Valley Forge as "a dreary kind of place and uncomfortably provided." During the training camp, the soldiers were trained more like a traditional army compared to the rag-tag bunch of militias they had been previously. Those who weren't skilled gunmen received target training. They all trained in hand-to-hand combat with bayonets and tomahawks.

Figure 46. Valley Forge

General George Washington and General Charles Lee commanded the army going into the Battle of Monmouth. Washington was facing criticism after his winter of non-engagement at Valley Forge. He was also criticized because other commanders in the Continental Army had found success in the previous months, but he had been defeated twice previously. Congress wanted him to keep pushing against the British.

The British soldiers at the time were led by Generals Clinton and Cornwallis, the same generals who had led the British victory at the Battle of Brooklyn. They numbered nearly 15,000 that day in Freehold Township, New Jersey. The Battle of Monmouth was the final battle of the Philadelphia Campaign, an attempt by the British to take control of all of Pennsylvania.

The British were interested in Pennsylvania because the Americans had recently moved their capital to Philadelphia. The capital was previously held in New York City, but after the British took control of New York, they were forced to flee. As the British successfully battled their way through Pennsylvania, the congress was forced to move from Philadelphia to York.

The Continental Army and the British forces met at Monmouth Courthouse in New Jersey as the British were marching back to New York from Pennsylvania. The British generals had been ordered to return to New York as a precaution after the French agreed to an alliance with the Americans.

6.1.1 BATTLE

Before the beginning of the battle, Washington had ordered Lee and a third of his army, about 700 men, to shadow the British as they marched across New Jersey to Sandy Hook. Lee attempted to launch an attack against the British at Monmouth, but he lacked confidence in his troops and information. Before the fighting began, Lee stalled at a bridge near Monmouth Courthouse; he was unsure if the British forces were still in the area. When he finally scouted ahead, after an hour of waiting, Lee spotted 2,000 British soldiers who made up the rearguard.

Shortly after the fighting began, Lee lost communication with his other officers. He didn't give anyone a plan. In a panic, the forces began to pull back without orders. Seeing that they were outnumbered, Lee officially pulled the troops back to a defensive position, giving the British a chance to take the advantageous position of offense. Lee chose to save as many soldiers as possible rather than seek victory. British General Henry Clinton, along with 8,000 soldiers, marched back toward the Monmouth Courthouse.

After botching the attack on the British rearguard at Monmouth Courthouse, Lee waited for reinforcement. Washington finally arrived with the remaining troops of the Continental Army. He and the troops marched upon fleeing soldiers and a chaotic Lee. None of the retreating soldiers could tell Washington the plan because there wasn't one. The British were winning for the moment.

| Henry Clinton | Nathaniel Greene | Anthony Wayne |

Figure 47. Generals Henry Clinton, Nathaniel Greene, and Anthony Wayne

Angry, Washington ordered Lee off the battlefield and instantly stripped him of his command. He demanded to know what caused the disorder and confusion. Lee could not give a satisfactory answer. In his place, Washington assigned General Nathaniel Greene, General Anthony Wayne, and General William Alexander.

Under new leadership, the Continental Army began to thrive in battle. All of the reinforcing troops made their way to Monmouth, so Washington began an assault with the full power of the Continental Army. He established defensive positions all across the hillside. The full power of the British Army was only a half-mile in front of the Continental Army.

General Anthony Wayne waited in the woods with three battalions of soldiers or at least 1,000 troops. They made up the rearguard while Washington commanded the front-facing troops.

Figure 48. Battle of Monmouth

The British, oblivious to Wayne's position, marched by unprotected. Wayne ordered his troops to fire. The training from the previous winter was apparent. Riflemen aimed at the British soldiers with great accuracy, attacking both flanks. After exchanging fire for several minutes, Wayne ordered his troops back to the main lines.

The fighting continued for several hours. The Continental's strong defensive position was evident as they drove the British back. The British launched a counterattack on Nathaniel Green's line but were repelled again under heavy gunfire. By the evening, the British needed to stop fighting. As Clinton ordered his right flank to retreat, Washington took advantage of the situation and launched an offensive attack on the British troops, the first one of the day, as the Continental Army had been in a defensive position all day.

At least 350 Continental soldiers attacked the British right flank. They succeeded in pushing back the British soldiers, and though they didn't cause heavy casualties, Washington regarded the fight as a psychological battle. The British right flank was notoriously feared by American soldiers, so to push them back was a morale boost.

The British continued to retreat. Some of Washington's generals believed they should have continued the attack while the British were tired, but Washington resisted. After a full day of battle in the hot June sun, even the Continental Army was tired. Both armies rested and regrouped. Though they had both suffered casualties, the Continental Army was weaker from heat exhaustion.

The next morning, the British troops were gone. They had escaped under cover of darkness back to their holding in New York City.

YouTube

Valley Forge (American Revolution) and Battle of Monmouth by History Heroes:

https://www.youtube.com/watch?v=MB-bogxmgJo

6.1.2 AFTERMATH

Figure 49. The capture of General Charles Lee

Some say that the Battle of Monmouth had no clear victor. Still, optimists can argue that the Continental Army was victorious in defending against the British and inflicting casualties despite a shaky start.

The British successfully returned to New York just in time to miss the arrival of the French coalition. They had lost roughly 358 soldiers in the Battle of Monmouth, though exact numbers are hard to pinpoint as several records indicate different death tolls.

The Battle of Monmouth potentially saved George Washington his career. After two defeats the previous year and a quiet winter that disappointed Congress, he finally had good news to report. He wrote a lengthy letter to Congress detailing the fight. It secured his position as Commander in Chief for the remainder of the war. The Americans viewed Monmouth as a solid victory.

But not all were celebrating after the battle. General Charles Lee was court-martialed shortly after the battle. He was charged with disobeying orders, conducting a shameful retreat, and disrespecting the Commander in Chief. It was true that Lee had written Washington a strongly worded, rude letter regarding his treatment after the battle. He also complained to anyone who would listen that George Washington was unfit to be the commander of the Army. His slandering would not go unpunished. Lee was found guilty on all three charges, but his punishment was simply removal from the Continental Army for one year.

6.2 BATTLE OF RHODE ISLAND
AUGUST 29, 1778

After the successful occupation of New York City, the British reallocated some troops to march to Rhode Island. The British then controlled Newport, Rhode Island, but they constantly fought to maintain the area's control. In late Spring of 1778, after the Americans received word that the French would assist them in the war, they began to plan their next major attack. The French sent 12 ships with more than 4,000 soldiers to the Continental forces.

Their first plan of attack was to sail for New York, but after further consideration, it was determined that the large French ships might not be able to fit in New York Harbor. So the plan was altered, and Newport, Rhode Island, was selected as the new point of attack.

General John Sullivan (Figure 51) of the Continental Army was given the command. Washington promised to send Sullivan 5,000 additional troops. The Battle of Rhode Island would be the first official battle that included the French as allies. The plan would require the French to join the attack from the west on land and assist the Continental Navy at sea.

The most contentious location in Newport was an island just off the coast, Aquidneck Island (Figure 50). There, Continental troops and British forces had been at odds since the original invasion in 1776. Sullivan chose this island as the starting point for this siege.

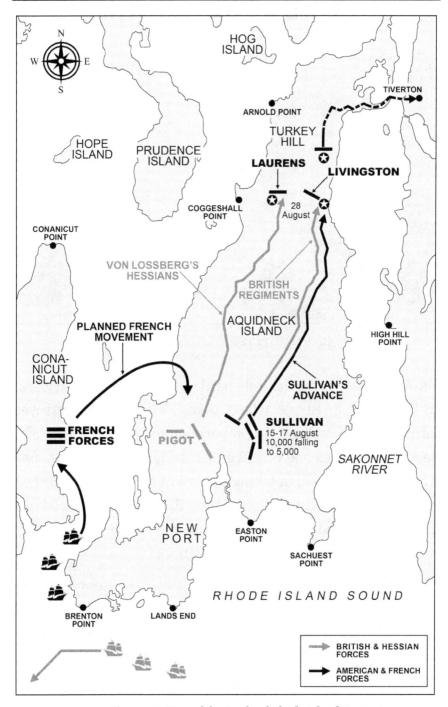

Figure 50. Map of the Battle of Rhode Island

6.2.1 BATTLE

General John Sullivan   General Charles d'Estaing

Figure 51. Generals John Sullivan and Charles d'Estaing

On August 29, 1778, the only battle of the Revolutionary War to be fought in Rhode Island began. The British destroyed farmlands and orchards in preparation for the fight, they also destroyed wagons and other resources in case the Continental Army was successful in taking control of Newport. The British had more than 7,000 soldiers at their disposal in Rhode Island, and they recalled those stationed in the farther-out zones in order to create a solid defensive position.

General Sullivan planned to split the troops so the Continental soldiers would attack Aquidneck Island from the east and the French would attack it from the west. French General Charles d'Estaing (Figure 51), who led the naval vessels, prepared to sail down the coast of Rhode Island to execute the plan.

Figure 52. Battle of Rhode Island

In the days leading up to the battle, the French Navy proved helpful. They fired at British ships until those ships ran aground and were unable to fight back. The British were forced to burn the ships to avoid capture. They also sank several ships just outside Newport Harbor, so the French ships could not sail any closer to Aquidneck Island.

As the navies fought and the British on land rearranged their position, Sullivan decided to seize Butt's Hill, where the British had previously held the high ground. Little did Sullivan realize he was about to be abandoned by this French naval assistance. Moreover, he was unaware of the sunken British ships that prevented d'Estaing from sailing any closer. Without that French aid at sea, it would be a much more difficult battle at Butt's Hill. They fired cannons into the British defensive position and the town for a few days, but they made very little progress.

Figure 53. General Francis Smith

The British added 4,000 soldiers to their forces in Newport while the American and French forces scrambled.

Sullivan was panicked. He ordered his troops to abandon the plan of taking Newport, but the British would not let him give up that easily. They were informed by defectors of the Continental Army of Sullivan's plans to give up. Instead of allowing the Americans to leave, they created a defensive position all across Rhode Island and prepared to attack.

British General Francis Smith (Figure 53) and Hessian General Friedrich Wilhelm von Lossberg were ordered to advance on the American left and right flanks, respectively. They did not expect these advancements to lead to a full-scale fight, but they were wrong.

British and American troops engaged in a heavy battle on both sides. Even without the French aid, the Continental Army continued to hold its ground against the British. Smith requested reinforcements from the main British coalition a few miles behind them. They were sent, but the extra manpower could not overtake the American position. So Smith decided against pursuing the attack on the left side. On the right, Lossberg had more success. He drove the Continental troops back from Turkey Hill all the way to their main forces. Unfortunately, this move meant that Lossberg's men were outnumbered. So they retreated back to Turkey Hill. Before long, the British were forced to cease the fighting because the Continental Army's position wasn't moving.

YouTube

Rhode Island in the Civil War by American Battlefield Trust: https://www.youtube.com/watch?v=mF6YfeZfwtw

6.2.2 AFTERMATH

The Battle of Rhode Island is not considered a true victory or defeat for either side. Though some may argue that because the Continental Army's goal of seizing Newport was not realized, they were defeated. The Continental troops marched out of Rhode Island, but they recovered all of their resources, artillery, and gunpowder.

In the end, at least 441 troops were dead. 260 British soldiers and 181 American soldiers had fallen. Nearly 17,000 total troops were involved in the conflict.

Regardless of the outcome of the Battle of Rhode Island, this battle was crucial for the political changes it signaled. This was the first battle that saw direct cooperation between the French and American forces. It was also the first battle that included a unit of African-American soldiers. This action was a significant step forward in the fight for African-American rights in the country, though it would be 90 more years until slavery was ended in the United States.

YouTube

History Brief: African Americans in the Revolution by Reading Through History:

https://www.youtube.com/watch?v=Z3p-uoo3CtE

6.3 SIEGE OF SAVANNAH
SEPTEMBER 19–OCTOBER 16, 1779

In 1778, the British chose to focus their efforts on the South. Despite earlier failures to capture Charleston, they still believed they could hold a powerful position supported by the Loyalists in the South. In the fall of 1778, the British successfully gained power in Savannah, Georgia. At that time, there was little resistance by local militia and poor colonial defenses. That victory in the South was a turning point for the British, who had been badly beaten in the North for many months.

Savannah had long been a gem of the South. The city was first established in 1734, and the colony of Georgia was named after British King George II. Colonizers hoped that by establishing Georgia as the southern border with South Carolina, they could protect the rest of the Thirteen Colonies from Spanish advances in Florida. Savannah is known as America's first "planned city." The settlers laid out 24 blocks for the town, many of which still exist today.

Long after the establishment of Savannah in the early 1700s, and after several months of British control in the city, the Patriots decided to attempt to retake the city. However, for their plan to work, the Continental Army knew they needed help from their French allies, specifically their strong naval force.

6.3.1 BATTLE & AFTERMATH

| General Benjamin Lincoln | General Augustine Prevost |

Figure 54. Generals Benjamin Lincoln and Augustine Prevost

The Continental Army had roughly 6,000 men stationed in Charleston, South Carolina, under the direction of General Benjamin Lincoln. Their French allies were sailing toward Georgia with 4,000 men and several warships. Lincoln felt sure that, with naval assistance, they had a shot at retaking Savannah. Meanwhile, the British had stationed 3,000 soldiers in Savannah under the direction of General Augustine Prevost. There were several hundred other British soldiers stationed around Southern Georgia, but General Prevost would need to recall them to Savannah quickly for their assistance.

Lincoln began the march to Savannah on September 11th, accompanied by 2,000 soldiers. He planned to meet up with the 4,000 French soldiers sailing toward Savannah and attack the British from both land and sea.

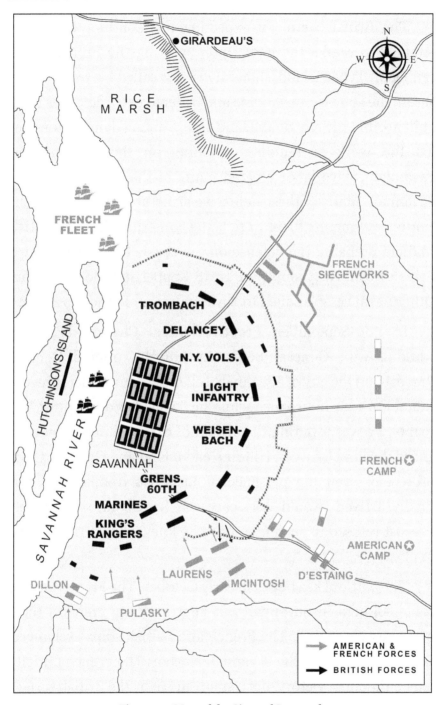

Figure 55. Map of the Siege of Savannah

The British were not expecting the Continental Army's attempt to retake the city. Upon spotting the French ships sailing off Tybee Island, General Prevost called his troops from across the state to consolidate and ordered extra defenses to be built around the city on the land side. Captain James Moncrief led the work of building redoubts on the land around Savannah. Slave labor created many of the defenses around Savannah. Many of these defensive structures were more than 1,000 feet long. As these were being constructed, other British soldiers prepared the defense on the coast. They boarded two British Royal Navy ships, the HMS Keppel and the Germaine. Other naval vessels sailed to Savannah from Florida to assist.

In mid-September, French General Charles d'Estaing, working with General Benjamin Lincoln, offered General Prevost and the city of Savannah a chance to surrender. Prevost called for a 24-hour truce while he "considered the offer." In reality, he was awaiting the arrival of extra reinforcements to guard the land between Hilton Head Island and Georgia. Once protected, even the presence of Lincoln's troops, who had finally arrived, would not scare the British into surrender. Prevost refused to surrender once he knew all his troops were in place.

The battle at sea began in early October. The French landed some soldiers in Savannah but kept a strong crew on their naval vessels as well. The French and British ships exchanged gunfire just outside the Savannah Harbor. The French initially felt confident of victory, but a smart move by the British turned the tides.

Figure 56. Siege of Savannah

The British intentionally sank one of their ships, HMS Rose, and set fire to another two, effectively blocking the entrance to Savannah's Harbor. The sunken ship would scrape the bottom of French vessels if they tried to sail over it, and the fire from the other two threatened to take French ships up in a blaze as well. Without an easy route into the city, the French fleet couldn't assist the Continental Army exactly as they had hoped. Instead, the French ships settled for shooting cannonballs into the city rather than the military defenses. They were shooting from quite a distance, but still effective. The French aimed well, and by the end of the siege, there wasn't a building left without damage. If the British were to keep the city, there wouldn't be much city left for them to keep.

The land battle began, against the advisement of both French and Continental commanders, on October 9, 1779. That morning was heavy with fog. Soldiers could hardly see where they were shooting, and many got lost in the swamps around the British defenses. The Continental Army and the French planned to overtake the British base at Spring Hill since they assumed this base was loosely guarded by a local militia and not the British Army.

When the fog lifted, the allies were dismayed to find that British soldiers were all around them. The trained shooters were easily finding and shooting their enemies. The French front line was exposed in the newly improved weather. Many French soldiers were shot, killed, or injured as they continued trying to overtake the base. There were dying soldiers scattered on the battlefield and filling up the trenches.

Subsequent waves of troops faced the same problems. When the second wave arrived, they found the first wave in disarray. No progress had been made to break through the British lines of defense.

Soon, d'Estaing called off his troops and left the Continental Army to fend for themselves. Within a week of brutal fighting, Lincoln also called off the attack. He led his remaining troops, not a large number, back to Charleston.

The Siege of Savannah is known as one of the bloodiest battles of the whole war. The British maintained control of Savannah for the remainder of the Revolutionary War. The Continental Army was not able to overtake the British forces during that time. After the 1779 Siege of Savannah, more than 1,000 Continental soldiers died. Only 150 British soldiers had fallen.

The defeat lifted British morale so much that they actually celebrated the victory. Celebratory cannons were launched in London.

The effects of the Siege of Savannah were relevant long after the Revolutionary War ended. The famous author Charles Dickens wrote about one character who participated in the battle and lost his arm. Even today, three United States Army units, the 118th FA, the 131st MP, and the 263rd ADA, can trace their routes to the Siege of Savannah. These three units are a part of 30 total United States Army units that can trace their origins back to the Revolutionary War.

Some portions of the battlefield remain today. Archeologists have restored the forts, found remains of artillery pieces, and established historical tours.

7. LATE BATTLES

Figure 57. Late Battles

The final battles of the war finally saw some significant American victories. The Battle of Yorktown was the official surrender of the British to the Continental Army, but a few minor fights still occurred in the final year before the Treaty of Paris was signed.

In the war's final years, the British focused on the Southern Strategy. They hoped that the Southern colonists benefited the most from trade with Britain and would produce a higher Loyalist population. Britain planned to take over Savannah, Georgia, and Charleston, South Carolina. While their battlefield strategies were successful in the South, their social strategy fell short. British soldiers alienated themselves from the traditionally Loyalist Southerners when they offered freedom to the enslaved people working on Southern plantations in exchange for their service in the British Army.

The plantation owners were not as quick to support the British efforts when they had taken their laborers away. The British also continued to rule with an iron fist, an attitude that further irritated the Southern colonists.

The tax-paying British citizens were tired of King George III's war in America. It was expensive and quickly depleted British resources. The British surrender was a combination of defeat in battle and pressure from the people back home.

To speed up the British surrender, George Washington refocused his war efforts. He continued to instruct his troops to avoid traditional battles, and they kept their focus on *guerrilla warfare*. Guerrilla warfare is a fighting style that relies on the element of surprise and quick attacks. This fighting style weakened the British forces and hurt morale, as they never knew when another attack was coming. The British were trained for traditional battle, not the strategy employed by the Continental Army. Washington knew that even though the British could outfight the Americans, they might not be able to outlast them regarding expenses, hunger, and lack of resources. In this way, dragging out the battles with smaller attacks was helping the Americans. But, not every fight was made by surprise. Despite the Continental Army's best efforts, they still had to face the British in a few traditional fights.

The fights in the war's final years include Charleston, Lenud's Ferry, Waxhaws, Yorktown, and Delaware Bay. The key leaders in these battles include George Washington, Benjamin Lincoln, Abraham Buford, Alexander Hamilton, and Joshua Barney.

7.1 SIEGE OF CHARLESTON
MARCH 29, 1780–MAY 12, 1780

The British had failed to take Charleston several times during the course of the war. First in 1776, then again in 1779. They would not be defeated a third time.

So far in the war, the British, with varying levels of success, had launched a Siege of Boston, a Philidelphia Campaign, and a Northern Campaign. With only a few years left to fight, they launched the Southern Campaign. They believed that the large Loyalist population in the South would help their war efforts. These battles would include the Siege of Charleston and Savannah. After numerous defeats, the British needed a few quick and easy wins to sway public favor. The war was getting expensive, and not everyone favored continuing the fighting back in Britain. The British planned to attack Charleston to use the port city as a base for future operations.

To help them win, the British promised slaves freedom in exchange for fighting against the Patriots. Black soldiers, known as Black Loyalists, flocked to the British cause from all around Charleston and the surrounding areas.

The Continental Army had seen recent victories. But the war in the North was a stalemate. In Charleston, they were led by General Benjamin Lincoln. There weren't many troops in Charleston for Lincoln to use. Washington declined to send reinforcements to Charleston because of the state of the war in the North. Lincoln was on his own with just 6,500 troops and was stuck with poorly maintained fortifications.

7.1.1 BATTLE & AFTERMATH

Figure 58. Siege of Charleston

British naval forces left New York City in December 1799 and intended to land directly in Charleston. The troops, commanded by General Henry Clinton, numbered nearly 14,000. They were aboard 14 warships and 90 smaller ships. Bad weather forced them to regroup in Savannah, delaying the invasion. In February 1780, they finally landed just a few miles south of Charleston on Simmons Island. At the same time, another British ship approached Charleston's Harbor. The isolated city was about to be surrounded.

General Benjamin Lincoln sent 350 troops north of Charleston to Moncks Corner to set up a strong defense before the British troops could reach the city. At the end of March 1780, British troops marched northwest of Charleston, and on April 1, 1780, they dug the first siege lines.

The meager Continental troops in the North resorted to loading their cannons with shards of glass and metal in order to preserve ammunition. They were running low on bullets and cannonballs. They shot the metal and glass at British defenses, trying to slow the construction of the siege lines or halt them.

A few days later, the first British ship arrived in Charleston's Harbor. The Continental Navy tried to obstruct the entrance, but they were outgunned by British artillery on board the ship. The ship sailed past the ruined Continental Navy and Fort Moultrie. The British offered Lincoln a chance to surrender, but Lincoln refused. If the British wanted to take Charleston, they were going to have to fight for it.

When the Patriots refused to surrender, the British began bombing the city. Cannons launched ammunition into the harbor and the seaside homes. Under cover of darkness, the city's government officials fled. It was just Lincoln and his troops that remained in Charleston.

At the same time, at Moncks Corner in the north, the British were reinforced with cavalry. They began fighting back with the 350 Continental soldiers that Lincoln had placed there. In no time, the British forces captured or killed all of Lincoln's troops at Moncks Corner. They also captured several hundred horses. By the next morning, Charleston was being bombed from the harbor and shot at by the British troops who had marched closer to the city limits.

Lincoln could not imagine a way out of Charleston, so he appealed to British General Henry Clinton. He offered to surrender the city if Clinton would allow the Continental troops to go free. Clinton declined.

Instead, the two armies fought in the streets of Charleston. The Continental soldiers succeeded in causing 50 British casualties in one fight thanks to their clever fighting strategies. Unfortunately, the loss of 50 soldiers did not stop the British path of destruction. Rather than give up, the British began bombing the city with "heated shells." These red-hot cannonballs caused fires to break out across the city. As the city burned, Lincoln was finally faced with no other option but to surrender, no matter what terms the British offered.

The Continental Army surrendered. They had fought bravely, but it was not enough to drive away the British forces.

After six long weeks of battle, General Benjamin Lincoln surrendered to the British. The American death toll was roughly 300. This loss of life was troubling to the Continental Army. It is considered one of the most costly defeats of the entire Revolutionary War. In the end, the British captured more than 5,000 prisoners and stole 311 cannons, 6,000 guns, tens of thousands of pieces of ammunition, and 50 ships. Most of those prisoners would die in captivity. The terms of surrender were harsh even for 1780.

The new British control of the South's largest port city was a difficult loss for the Continental Army to overcome. They were defeated several more times in smaller battles in the South. It would take a full year of fighting for the Continental Army to win back South Carolina.

7.2 BATTLE OF LENUD'S FERRY
MAY 6, 1780

Figure 59. Location of Lenud's Ferry

The Battle of Lenud's Ferry was fought at a crossing point of the Santee River. Leading up to the battle, British General Henry Clinton had ordered various sections of his troops to place themselves at the escape points of Charleston. He knew that the Continental Army and leaders under General Benjamin Lincoln would need to leave the city at some point, and he wasn't planning on letting them get far.

While the British fought the battle of Charleston as a whole, they also planned these smaller skirmishes to weed out

Figure 60. Lieutenant Colonel William Washington

every Continental soldier in South Carolina. Lincoln was fighting in Charleston with nearly 6,500 troops. He knew the Continental Army couldn't sustain a loss in any other areas during this time.

Lieutenant Colonel William Washington (Figure 60) was leading his troops north of the Santee River when they encountered 18 British soldiers patrolling near the river. They took all 18 soldiers hostage. Later, the Patriots took another group of British soldiers hostage after they were discovered at a nearby plantation. This action would incite war in just a few days. Nearby, British General Banastre Tarleton (Figure 61) discovered what had happened to his patrolling troops and made plans to take revenge on Washington and the Continental Army.

7.2.1 BATTLE

Colonel Abraham Buford   General Banastre Tarleton

Figure 61. Colonel Abraham Buford and General Banastre Tarleton

Lieutenant Colonel William Washington planned to connect his troops with the forces under Colonel Abraham Buford on the other side of the Santee River. Buford was commanding about 350 soldiers. Both coalitions had been a part of the forces fighting at Moncks Corner a few months earlier. But British General Banastre Tarleton would not allow Washington's actions to go unchecked.

Tarleton and his troops, about 150 men, followed Washington's coalition to the Santee River in secret. Then, they opened fire.

The Continental Army was completely taken by surprise; worse, their allies and Buford were stuck on the other side of the river and couldn't offer any help.

Aidless, the Continental Army quickly fell to the British Army. Several soldiers were killed, and even more were taken hostage, but some managed to flee by jumping into the river and swimming across. Some who chose to swim also drowned in the rapids as this was not an easy river to forge. The river was fast and wide, and only the best swimmers made it across. These swimmers included Washington.

It was a victory for the British Army and proved that movement around Charleston would be difficult for the Patriots.

7.2.2 AFTERMATH

The defeat of the forces at Lenud's Ferry totally destroyed the Continental cavalry. Beating Washington's troops at the Battle of Lenud's Ferry was the boost the British needed at this point in the war. There were zero British casualties. They collected horses, ammunition, and weapons from the defeated Patriots. Tarleton's troops especially needed the extra horses as they were struggling to move quickly through the colony. They were also able to free most of the British prisoners that Washington had imprisoned.

Meanwhile, the Continental Army lost more than 40 soldiers. Shortly after this battle at Lenud's Ferry, Lincoln was forced to surrender at Charleston. It signaled a terrifying tipping point in favor of the British.

With the tides in their favor, Tarleton and his 150 troops chased Buford north and fought them at the Buford Massacre, just before the North Carolina border. At the end of that battle, there were no more factions of the Continental Army in South Carolina.

7.3 BATTLE OF WAXHAWS
MAY 29, 1780

Figure 62. Location of Waxhaws Battle

The Battle of Waxhaws is also known as Buford's Massacre. In the weeks leading up to this battle, the Patriots had been defeated in Charleston and the surrounding areas. Their stand under Colonel Abraham Buford would be their last.

Buford had nearly 400 troops with him and two six-pound cannons. He was marching away from Charleston, South Carolina. British General Charles Cornwallis had heard of Buford's presence and decided to send General Banastre Tarleton to engage with Buford and his men.

Tarleton made up the 150-mile gap between the two armies in record time, and he met Buford on the border of South and North Carolina, a land known as the Waxhaws.

As he marched closer, Tarleton sent a messenger to Buford's troops, asking them to surrender. Buford refused Tarleton's offer, sent his heavy artillery pieces ahead so as not to lose them in a battle, and lined up his remaining troops in a field to prepare for battle.

According to the rumor on the battlefield, while Buford lined up his troops and Tarleton prepared for battle, the British forces intercepted a Continental Army medic. They also captured part of the Continental rearguard and brutally killed them.

7.3.1 BATTLE & AFTERMATH

Figure 63. Battle of Waxhaws

In comparison to Buford's strategy for patience, the British were taking an aggressive approach. As soon as they were in formation, Tarleton's troops rushed at the Continental soldiers so quickly that they hardly had time to fire their guns. Had the Continental soldiers fired sooner, they may have had more time to reload their weapons before the British came within striking distance. Instead, the three columns of the British offense broke through the American line in minutes. The battle was brutal and bloody. Many American survivors claimed they were attacked and killed as they tried to surrender.

The exact accounts of the battle vary. Most American chroniclers claim that the Continental Army wasn't resisting; they attempted to surrender. Yet, Tarleton and the British troops attacked soldiers who did not even hold weapons.

Buford sent forward a signal to surrender, but the white flag of surrender was refused. Continental troops attempted to flee, but most were captured and then killed by British troops.

Tarleton's horse was shot out from underneath him. As the horse fell, it trapped Tarleton underneath its heavy body. He was unable to effectively lead for the remainder of the battle, and this may account for why his troops continued after the surrender flag was flown. Battle only ceased when there were hardly any Continental troops left alive.

Buford made it out of the battle alive, and thank goodness, as the tales he told would electrify the Continental Army commanders. He was not joined by many Continental soldiers, though. If Buford's testimony of the battle was to be believed, it violated the "rules for war."

The British were victorious at the Battle of Waxhaws. They lost only five soldiers and left with 14 wounded. However, Tarleton, who was known for being an aggressive commander, was now labeled a butcher by the Continental Army.

The American casualties were heavy. There were at least 113 dead soldiers, and more than 200 soldiers were wounded. The British took some prisoners, but the Continental Army coined the term *"Tarleton's quarter,"* meaning take no prisoners.

Despite the loss at the Battle of Waxhaws, the Americans were able to create something useful. A *propaganda* campaign. Propaganda is a form of advertising that persuades an audience to further the creator's agenda. In this case, the creators were the Patriots and Founding Fathers, who wanted the rest of America to rally support around their soldiers. They needed them to see and believe the atrocities in the Battle of Waxhaws and finally give up support for the British.

The propaganda that circulated after the Battle of Waxhaws was influential in turning some Loyalists' favor toward the Patriots' cause. The Patriots used newspaper articles, drawings of battles, and plain word of mouth to sway public opinion toward the British. Thanks to their efforts, the anti-British sentiment grew overnight.

As the battles in the South continued, stories say that many militia groups would yell, "Remember the Waxhaws," as they defeated smaller coalitions of British troops and Loyalist allies. However, no amount of skirmishes could loosen the British position in the South. They maintained their power in both South Carolina and Georgia for the remainder of the war.

7.4 BATTLE OF COWPENS
JANUARY 17, 1781

Figure 64. Location of Cowpens

The countryside of South Carolina was a heavily divided area. The colonists who called the area home were basically engaged in their own civil war over the question of American independence. The Patriots and the Loyalists each had formed their own mini militias, enacting raids on each other and pitting neighbors and families against each other.

The British were adding fuel to the fire. George Washington, sensing a chance to turn the tides of the war in the South, sent General Nathanael Greene to South Carolina in hopes of organizing the Patriot forces. Greene entered the fire, ready to make some changes. His first order was to split the Patriot forces in half. He sent one group of roughly 1,000 soldiers, commanded by General Daniel Morgan, to cut off British supply lines near the Catawaba River. These American troops were a mixed group of trained Continental soldiers and southern Patriot militia members. The British would not let that move go unanswered. They sent General Tarleton, who had just received his reputation from the Battle of Waxhaws, to meet Morgan and the Continental Army. Tarleton also commanded about 1,000 troops.

7.4.1 BATTLE & AFTERMATH

Figure 65. Battle of Cowpens

Tarleton chased Morgan through the South Carolina countryside. His aggressive pursuit was a misguided move at the time because he did not know how many troops Morgan was leading. Morgan, however, knew that the two sides were evenly matched. He attempted to make camp and prepare his troops for battle, but the quickly approaching British forced him to retreat to a cow pasture a few miles back.

The land around the Cowpens was open, with rolling hills and little tree coverage. The riflemen on either side would have little to no natural defenses, but Morgan spotted a valley that was perfect for hiding cavalry forces. He gathered his troops around the campfire and began to formulate a plan. He feared that the untrained Continental troops could flee in the face of the infamous Tarleton, so he needed a foolproof plan for the battle that would encourage his troops and take advantage of the British weaknesses.

In the end, Morgan organized his troops for a head-on battle but left his flanks seemingly unguarded. He hoped the British would take the bait.

As Tarleton and his troops advanced over the next hill, Morgan ordered the riflemen in the front line to shoot British commanders. Without commanders, the British troops would lack order and direction. These riflemen fired their guns with incredible accuracy, and the commanders fell. The next row of Patriot militiamen fired two rounds of gunfire into the British line, causing heavy casualties, before falling back. The British mistakenly assumed that this fallback was a true retreat. In reality, it was to expose the final, third line of Morgan's troops. The third line was made up of mostly trained Continental soldiers who continued to fire into the British lines.

Many British soldiers were killed in the initial exchange of gunfire, but the few remaining troops continued to press forward under Tarleton's orders. As they advanced, the Americans brought out the bayonets. The hand-to-hand combat was brutal, and the Continental troops continued slaughtering the British. They even succeeded in breaking the British lines to steal two of their cannons.

Sensing defeat was near, the front lines of the British coalition laid down their guns in surrender. Morgan then sent his cavalry to the back lines of Tarleton's troops which included Tarleton himself. The Continental cavalry easily overwhelmed the remaining British troops.

Brutal fighting with guns and sabers destroyed the British soldiers, and those soldiers who tried to flee were easily captured by the Continental cavalry. One cavalryman, William Washington, took on fighting Tarleton himself. They clashed swords, fighting for several minutes until Tarleton shot Washington's horse out from under him. In the moments of Washington escaping from under his horse, the remaining British troops fled. It was a victory for the Continental forces.

The British suffered hefty casualties in the Battle of Cowpens. More than 800 soldiers were killed or captured, leaving barely 200 from Tarleton's original force alive. The Continental Army only lost 149 soldiers in the fighting.

Morgan fled north with his troops and newly acquired British prisoners. There he met back up with Nathanael Greene and the other half of the Continental Army. The Battle of Cowpens would be his final battle as he retired from duty shortly afterward.

General Charles Cornwallis, the British commander in Charleston, South Carolina, realized he was losing ground in South Carolina. Rather than remain, he chose to pursue the Americans north. They skirmished a few times in North Carolina before the British ultimately withdrew to Yorktown, Virginia, where they would finally be defeated in the final battle of the Revolutionary War.

7.5 BATTLE OF YORKTOWN
SEPTEMBER 28–OCTOBER 19, 1781

Figure 66. Location of Yorktown

By 1781, the Revolutionary War was also growing unpopular with American citizens. After six years of fighting, it was growing to be a very expensive endeavor for both the British and the Americans. The British were not only fighting the Continental Army in America, but their war had expanded in Europe too, where they were fighting France and Spain.

Both sides believed they needed one major victory in order to put an end to the war. The Battle of Yorktown would be that decisive battle.

Marshal Comte de Rochambeau   Lt. General Francois de Grasse

Figure 67. Comte de Rochambeau and François Joseph de Grasse

There were two choices for the potential last major battle of the war. The Continental Army could strike the British in New York City, or they could attack further south in Yorktown. The British only had a few strongholds left along the coast. In New York City, there remained the majority of their reinforcements and the central holding for all the British resources. Meanwhile, Cornwallis had stopped in Yorktown to resupply and wait for reinforcements. He had only 9,000 soldiers. General George Washington and his French commanding ally Marshal Jean-Baptiste de Vimeur (Comte de Rochambeau), debated which location to set their final battle. Washington favored New York City, but Rochambeau favored Yorktown. Ultimately, the Patriots decided that attacking Yorktown had the highest chance of success. If Washington's plan to surround Cornwallis in Yorktown was going to work, he needed the French Navy commanded by Lieutenant General

Francois Joseph de Grasse (Figure 67) to be successful. This decision prompted the largest movement of Continental troops in the entire war, nearly 20,000 soldiers marched hundreds of miles to fight in the Battle of Yorktown.

In the days before the battle, the allies got word that the British Royal Navy was coming to reinforce Cornwallis. Rochambeau sent a message to de Grasse and asked him to meet the British Navy in the Chesapeake Bay. De Grasse complied and immediately began sailing north to the Chesapeake Bay, Maryland, Virginia. He had more than 4,000 soldiers and sailors under his command. They sailed aboard 37 warships.

The engagement between the two navies on September 5, 1781, became known as the Battle of the Capes. It is considered one of the most critical naval battles in the United States' history, and technically the Americans did not even participate in the fight. The entire sea battle only lasted two hours and thirty minutes.

The British got word of the French's movements but were unaware of the final destination, the Chesapeake Bay or New York Harbor. This confusion slowed their response, so when British ships finally reached the Chesapeake Bay, the French had already been anchored off the coast for several days. As soon as the British sailed into the Chesapeake Bay, they got into battle formation. No time would be wasted.

As the British got into formation, the French were still unloading their ships and not paying attention to the incoming fleet. When de Grasse finally saw that the British were sailing closer, he was forced to rush his sailors aboard in a moment of chaos. The French fleet began to raise anchor and sail into the bay. Thankfully, the British were not quick enough to take advantage of the French's chaotic assembly.

Cannon fire shot through the sky, and both fleets aimed at one another. Cannonballs were hurled into the sides of ships and splashed into the sea. The volley of artillery fire between the two sides continued for two hours. The fleets disengaged at sunset to assess their damages. The British lost six ships, but the French lost only two. The British commanders were hesitant to continue fighting, realizing that they did not have enough resources to take down the French, they sailed away in the night.

The French Navy's defeat of the British Navy left Cornwallis without the reinforcements he desperately needed, opening the stage for the land Battle for Yorktown.

7.5.1 BATTLE

Figure 68. Battle of Yorktown

The whole battle would take three weeks to complete. On the first day, September 28, 1781, the American and French allied troops finally ended their march for hundreds of miles outside Yorktown.

Cornwallis had erected several defensive forts outside the city and kept his exhausted soldiers both in the forts and in the city. The Continental Army surrounded the city, and Washington sent a covert team to assess the British defenses. There were seven redoubts around the city, connected with a chain of earth-built defenses and batteries. The Americans concluded that these defenses would be easy to subdue.

The American and French troops built their trenches outside of Yorktown. Trench warfare allowed them to get as close as possible to the British while avoiding hand-to-hand combat and maintaining a solid defense. As the Continental troops inched closer, the British opened fire. They were running low on resources inside the British defenses, but they attempted to use their remaining ammunition to stop the building of the trenches. They were unsuccessful. All around them, the Continental Army and their allies were adequately defended and ready for war.

The Continental Army constantly fired cannons at Yorktown and the British defenses. All day and all night, cannons boomed into the British line. General George Washington was said to have ceremoniously lit the first cannon to strike the city. The British were out of any ammunition that could have defended against these attacks, so they were forced to wait out the storm of cannonballs. In the meantime, they endured heavy casualties. Cornwallis pulled back his troops from the city's outer defenses, hoping to wait for reinforcements. He left soldiers in two of the redoubts as a final line of defense. General Henry Clinton had promised him support, but it took them a week to march to Yorktown.

After a few days of heavy cannon fire, the Continental Army took over the two remaining British forts surrounding Yorktown. They built a new trench line even closer to the city after these captures were complete. Bad weather disguised their trench work so the British could not see the enemy coming nearer. It is said that George Washington even helped to dig the trenches. Winning the Battle of Yorktown would be an all-hands-on-deck effort. They loaded hundreds of guns and artillery pieces into the trenches. Continental engineers plotted out the best positions for cannons.

By October 12th, they had moved forward 400 yards closer to the British. In their improved position, the Continental Army began to shoot their hundreds of guns at the British defenses. The gunfire lasted all night long with no breaks for the British to assess their damages. It was a disastrous blow to the British in Yorktown. Many soldiers began to flee for their lives.

To really seal in victory, the Continental Army began to plan a secret attack on the British forts. They used a surprising tactic in this attack. They did not load their guns before storming forward in hopes that they were quieter without the loaded weapons. The codeword for the troops to begin the attack was "Rochambeau," the name of the allied French Marshal.

"Rochambeau" was whispered between the troops on the night of October 14, 1781. A small group of Continental soldiers attacked a fort to the north of Yorktown as a diversion. With the British defending that fort, Alexander Hamilton and 400 soldiers could carry out the actual attack further south. The Americans climbed the fort walls and fought in violent, hand-to-hand combat with the British soldiers. Despite the tense fight, the Americans were victorious and only lost 34 out of 400 soldiers in the attack.

The same night, the French soldiers attacked another fort and were equally successful. After October 14th, the British were surrounded on three sides, and the Continental Army and their allies took control of a substantial amount of the British weaponry from the forts.

In a desperate attempt to fight his way out, Cornwallis attempted a counterattack. He was unsuccessful.

On October 17, 1781, the British waved a white flag. They wanted to surrender. However, George Washington would not make it that easy for them. On October 19, 1781, when the two generals met in the middle, Washington denied Cornwallis the surrender because the British did not allow the Americans to surrender in Charleston the year prior. In a formal surrender, the defeated army would be allowed to march off the battlefield with the enemy's national anthem playing and white flags raised along with their national flag. Instead, Washington demanded the British Army leave the field with no flags, and they were to play a British tune. Some say they chose "The World Turned Upsidedown."

YouTube

28th September 1781: The Siege of Yorktown begins in the American Revolutionary War by HistoryPod:
    https://www.youtube.com/watch?v=BPFZ88XIv9M

Battle of Yorktown (American Revolution) by History Heroes:
    https://www.youtube.com/watch?v=Mg7GA_aBeHw

7.5.2 AFTERMATH

In the end, the Continental Army was victorious over the British in this final major battle of the Revolutionary War. More than 8,000 British soldiers were killed, wounded, or captured in the fighting. The Americans lost only a few hundred.

Their defeat at the Battle of Yorktown was the defeat of the British Army overall. They were not able to recover their forces after this loss. They would lose the American colonies too.

The British Army was one of the strongest in the world but was defeated by amateur militias in their own colonies. This war was also the first instance of colonies uniting to fight for independence from their colonizers. Several more territories would take a page from America's book in their wars in the years to come.

A few months after the Battle of Yorktown, the British government passed a bill allowing them to make peace with America. It would be two more years before the final peace treaty was signed, and a few mild skirmishes broke out in those two years, but the Battle of Yorktown signifies the major end to the war.

7.6 BATTLE OF JOHNSTOWN
OCTOBER 25, 1781

Figure 69. Location of Johnstown

The British were not kind to the land in New York that they had occupied for several years. Since the Battle of Brooklyn in 1776, the British had burned fields, harassed merchants from nearby territories, killed civilians, and raided resources from towns in upstate New York.

New York Governor George Clinton (Figure 70) requested assistance from the Continental Army and local militias to get the British treatment of locals under control and fix the supply lines between towns, forts, and settlements in the valley.

| George Clinton | Marinus Willet | John Ross |

Figure 70. Governor George Clinton, Colonel Marinus Willet, and Major John Ross

Colonel Marinus Willet was up to the task. He led troops into the valley.

Willet patrolled the valley for several months, and his troops engaged in minor skirmishes with the Loyalists and British in the area, but the largest battle was yet to come. In October of 1781, just after the Battle of Yorktown, a larger coalition of British troops, allies, and Loyalists entered the valley. Major John Ross (Figure 70) was leading them. They were spotted by two Continental Army scouts who spread the word of the British presence to Willett and the other troops.

7.6.1 BATTLE & AFTERMATH

Willett scrambled to assemble the troops because the British weren't wasting any time. They were burning towns and killing civilians as they marched toward Willett's position. The two forces met right outside Johnstown.

The American troops were outnumbered. They had roughly 400 soldiers, and the British had over 700 soldiers. Willett split the Americans into two groups. One would circle to fight the British from the rear, and the other would attack directly. The fighting quickly began. British and American troops exchanged gunfire back and forth on their front lines. The only cannon on the battlefield belonged to the Continental Army, but it was captured and recaptured by both sides multiple times.

As Continental soldiers and militiamen began to fall or flee, Willett worried that they would be defeated. Just when hope was beginning to wane, the second group of soldiers appeared from behind the British and began to attack from the rear just as Willett had ordered. The British were completely surrounded.

At that moment, two fights were occurring at once, the one between Willett's men and the British front lines and the one between the second group of Continental soldiers and the British rear lines. The British were overwhelmed, and they fled to a nearby hill.

The next day the British began to march out of Mohawk Valley, but they were followed by Willett and the Continental

Army all the way to their base at Oneida Lake. Small skirmishes broke out here and there between the troops, but the large-scale fight was over.

The Continental Army's success in Mohawk Valley effectively ended the reign of British violence in the area. They surrendered and retreated just as the British troops in Yorktown were surrendering. With the threat neutralized in the area, Willett and his men were able to return home.

There were only a few dozen killed between the two sides, but the Continental Army took over 30 British soldiers prisoner after the Battle of Johnstown.

7.7 BATTLE OF DELAWARE BAY
APRIL 8, 1782

Figure 71. Location of Delaware Bay

Though the Battle of Yorktown had ended a few months prior, small skirmishes still broke out between the Americans and the British, specifically the British Loyalists who remained in the country.

Loyalists had a reputation for attacking Patriot ships that went out to sea, as they did on April 8, 1782, in the Battle of Delaware Bay.

Attacking ships had become a common practice as the Americans attempted to spread their trading wings with other countries for the first time. During the time of British control, the colonies were only allowed to trade with Great Britain. Now that they had declared independence, they were free to trade with whatever country offered the highest bid. America was rich in natural resources that Europe lacked. Tobacco, cotton, wood, and some products that were expensive commodities in Europe. Because of the hostile British attitude towards American trade, most merchant ships required naval protection when sailing in and out of American harbors at Charleston, Boston, New York, Savannah, and other major cities.

7.7.1 BATTLE & AFTERMATH

Figure 72. Captain Joshua Barney

Captain Joshua Barney was assigned to the Hyder Ally, a warship meant to protect merchants sailing out of the harbor with their goods. The Hyder Ally was joined by two ships, General Greene and Charming Sally. While these warships guarded a convoy of merchants, they were spotted by three British ships: The HMS Quebec, General Monk, and Fair American. One of these ships had earlier been captured by the Continental Army.

The merchant ships were ordered back into the Bay by Barney. Soon, the Fair American attempted to pursue the merchant ships back into the harbor, and the HMS Quebec blocked the entrance to the bay. The General Monk directly approached the Hyder Ally.

Figure 73. Battle of Delaware Bay

The men aboard Hyder Ally quaked. General Monk had double the weaponry that the Hyder Ally had on board. However outmatched Hyder Ally was, it would have to fight alone because most of the other ships had run aground.

Barney was determined not to show any fear. As they sailed closer to the General Monk, he ordered all the cannons and guns to be loaded, and then when they were in firing range, he signaled for the fire to rain down. Dozens of cannons and guns shredded the masts and sails of the General Monk in that first assault.

In a move that would win him the battle, Barney called over his first mate, "I am going to shout out my next order for the enemy's benefit but follow my next order by the rule of the contrary." When Barney yelled, loud enough for the captain of the General Monk to hear, that he wanted the crew to turn the ship to the left, they did as he commanded, the opposite. They turned the ship to the right and took the General Monk off guard. The Hyder Ally was then positioned to attack the unprotected side of the enemy ship.

The ships sailed close enough together for the sailors aboard Hyder Ally to engage in hand-to-hand combat with the sailors aboard the General Monk. They went aboard. In close quarters, the fighting was brutal. The sailors fought for nearly an hour before the highest-ranking British sailor left alive and called for a surrender.

There were 20 dead British soldiers and more than 30 wounded. On the American side, only four were dead and a dozen wounded. The Battle of Delaware Bay was yet another American victory.

As Barney sailed both ships back into the bay, he discovered the merchant ships docked and safe back at the harbor. The Continental Army claimed and refurbished the General Monk, renaming the ship General Washington. A few months later, when the Treaty of Paris was signed between Britain and America, it would be the only Continental warship still active in the waters.

8. AFTERMATH OF THE REVOLUTIONARY WAR

Thomas Jefferson	John Jay
John Adams	David Hartley

Figure 74.Thomas Jefferson, John Jay, John Adams, and David Hartley

It took two years for the war to wind down. From the moment of the British surrender at the Battle of Yorktown in 1781 to the signing of the Treaty of Paris in 1783, there were a few minor skirmishes, like the Battle of Delaware Bay.

The Treaty of Paris, named because it was negotiated and signed in Paris, France, was the peace agreement between Great Britain and their former colonies, which would soon become the United States of America. It also involved France, Spain, and the Netherlands. France had allied itself with the colonies partway through the war. The signing of this agreement brought the United States to the main stage of international relations.

Thomas Jefferson, John Jay, and John Adams (Figure 74) represented the colonies during negotiations and the signing of the treaty. David Hartley represented Britain. The men had many objectives they wanted to achieve. They didn't win every point they were hoping for, but some of the major political victories included an agreement that Great Britain would recognize America's independence and a land agreement with France that would allow the Americans to expand west.

When Jefferson, Jay, and Adams returned to North America, there was lots of work still to be done. No official government was set up in the colonies, and lots of debate about the right way to run the country. In the immediate aftermath of the Declaration of Independence, the individual states had drawn up State Constitutions. These documents helped citizens of each state determine the law, but larger ideas about the union and who would lead were yet to be determined.

The states had united under the Articles of Confederation in 1777 to defeat the British by working together. These articles were finally ratified in 1781. According to the Articles of Confederation, each state was allowed one vote or representative in the Continental Congress. But when the war was over, they were still just 13 individual states, each with its own government and separate entities. Moreover, paying for war caused all states to fall into an economic slump.

The Second Continental Congress lacked the money it needed to get anything done. According to the Articles of Confederation, Congress could not levy taxes, and all financial details were left to the individual state governments. So they requested tax money from the states, but because each state had different laws, the amounts of money the Congress received were inconsistent and not nearly enough. Along with lacking financial authority, Congress was also not allowed to have a say in international trade or establish a judiciary system. So they needed to come up with a different system.

Along with changes to the government structure at the time, significant social and economic changes took place within America. Thanks to the establishment of state governments, more everyday men could participate in local and state-level politics. This was a massive change from the past British-enforced governors and far-away parliament. There were also new trade opportunities. When Britain ruled America, they were locked in trade with only Britain. From there, Britain would trade American natural resources with other countries.

As a free country, America could trade with France, Spain, Britain, and any other country. These new trade opportunities gave the economy a boost, not nearly enough to solve the debt problem created by the war, but it was better than nothing. They also created domestic trade and new manufacturing opportunities as more Americans traveled west. These trailblazers would need materials to settle lands west of the 13 original colonies so that demand improved American manufacturing and internal economy.

The Articles of Confederation ruled the 13 independent states for five years after the Revolutionary War ended. Those five years were filled with change and turmoil, and creating a document to replace the Articles wasn't easy, and it took time to come together.

8.1 CONSTITUTION OF THE UNITED STATES OF AMERICA

In 1787 the Constitutional Convention first met in Philadelphia, Pennsylvania. They gathered at Independence Hall, where the Declaration of Independence had been signed into law 11 years before. There were 55 representatives at the convention. They represented 12 of the 13 states. Rhode Island refused to participate on the grounds that it did not support a central government ruling over the states. The 55 representatives were all men, eight were signers of the Declaration of Independence, six were signers of the Articles of Confederation, nearly all had served in the Continental Army during the war, and they held positions that ranged from lawyers to farmers. Most were in their 30s or 40s, but Benjamin Franklin was the oldest representative at 81. James Madison acted as the secretary for the convention, taking detailed notes that would later help us understand what happened at these closed-door meetings. George Washington was unanimously voted President of the United States.

Originally, these representatives gathered to amend the Articles of Confederation. However, they realized they wanted an entirely new form of government. The convention would reconvene several times throughout 1787 to debate the details. Finally, the first draft of the United States Constitution was proposed. It suggested a democratic republic, the first of its kind. It was written by James Madison, with help from several other delegates, including Alexander Hamilton and Thomas Jefferson.

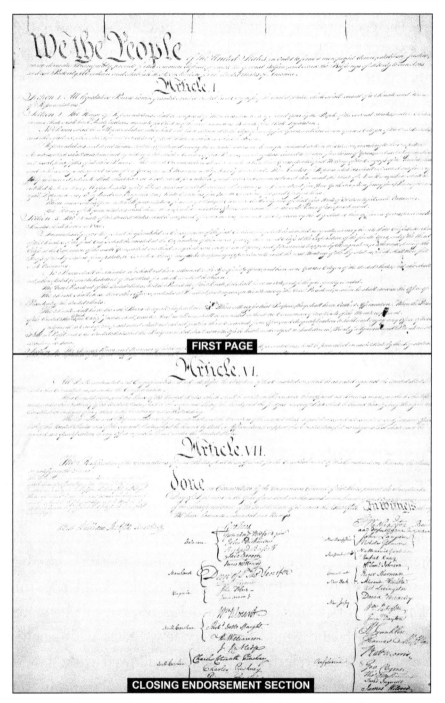

Figure 75. The Constitution of the United States of America

The Constitution would unite the 13 states into one nation and came with a lengthy Bill of Rights that would give the citizens of the country certain, undeniable rights; the freedom of speech is one of these. The document assigned one central federal government that would be in control of the treasury, taxes, and the military. The Bill of Rights was created as a way to ease anxieties over centralized federal power. For some, a federal power too closely resembled the monarchy they had left in Britain. The Constitution set up three branches of the federal government; the Executive Branch, the Judicial Branch, and the Legislative Branch. They called it a system of checks and balances. This document established the Congress as a part of the Legislative Branch. Congress would write the laws. They also established the position of the president, a figure who would use his executive powers to sign bills into law, command the army, and represent the country. The president made up the Executive Branch. The Judicial Branch was to be made up of several judges who would enforce the laws.

Apart from these government structures, the Constitution laid out the laws around taxes, slavery, and the states' rights. The states' rights were a hot topic of debate at the conventions. States with large populations favored a plan to have a number of representatives relative to the state's population. Under this plan, New York would have many delegates, but smaller states like Rhode Island would have very few. States with smaller population sizes preferred a system that allowed every state to have an equal number of representatives present in the government.

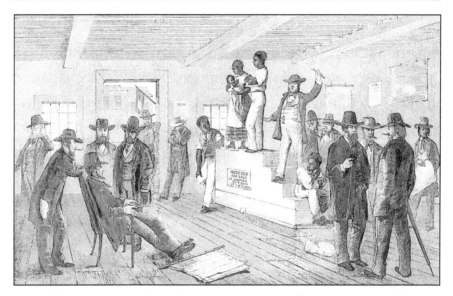

Figure 76. Slavery in the United States

To rectify the issue of delegates, the states created the Senate, or the upper house, which would allow two representatives from every state, and the House of Representatives, or the lower house, which would allow a number of representatives proportionate to the population of the state. These two groups created Congress. Both groups had to pass laws in order for them to be moved to the president's desk.

The Consitution also dissolved many of the British traditions that were still alive in America. For example, the Constitution stipulated that elections would be held for government positions. However, it left the decision of who could vote up to the states. That meant that in 1787, the only voting citizens were white, land-owning men. The law left out women, people of color, and anyone who didn't own land.

Slavery was another issue that earned lots of time and attention while the representatives crafted the Constitution. In 1787, slavery was legal and common. It wouldn't be outlawed in the United States for 78 more years. The Southern States, which relied on slavery more than those in the North to run their plantations, argued that the issue of slavery should be left out of the Constitution. They wanted to leave it up to the individual state governments to decide whether or not they allowed the practice. There was also the dilemma of how to count a state's population. The Southern States appeared to have more citizens if they agreed to count the slaves as a part of the population. The population would have a direct impact on the number of representatives a state was given.

As a compromise, the representatives agreed that each enslaved person would be counted as three-fifths of a white person. This policy seems inhumane by today's standards, but the world was a much different place in 1787. The representatives also agreed not to return to the issue of outlawing slavery at the federal level until 1808. That bought the South 20 years to continue to buy and sell enslaved people and benefit economically from free labor. Without these compromises around slavery, many of the Southern States would not have joined the union.

After intense debate and editing, the final draft of the Constitution was signed by 39 delegates on September 17, 1787. Finally, on June 21, 1788, the Constitution was ratified and became the official governing document of the United States of America.

Figure 77. The signing of the Constitution

In order to gain the approval they needed, Alexander Hamilton, John Jay, and James Madison wrote "The Federalist Papers." These papers are a set of 85 essays defending the Constitution. They were published in newspapers all across the country, trying to sway public opinion of the Constitution. In them, Jay, Hamilton, and Madison explained how the new Constitution would work and broke things down into ordinary language for citizens who weren't politically inclined. Originally, these papers were published anonymously.

Those who supported the Constitution became known as Federalists, thanks in part to the name given to Hamilton, Jay, and Madison's publications. Those who opposed the Constitution were known as Anti-Federalists. In many ways, these designations became the first two political parties of the United States.

The first states to ratify the Constitution were Delaware, Pennsylvania, New Jersey, Georgia, and Connecticut. Later, in 1788, it was ratified in Massachusetts, Maryland, and South Carolina. The ninth state to ratify was New Hampshire on June 21, 1788. The Bill of Rights was ratified on December 15, 1791. This document's creation was essential because it convinced some states, like Massachusetts, to approve the Constitution as a whole.

This Constitution continues to be the living document that governs the United States today. It has added 27 amendments, including laws for women's rights, minority rights, and term limits. But at its core, the Constitution we rely on today is the same set of governing guidelines that the Founding Fathers believed in during the Revolutionary War.

YouTube

The Making of the American Constitution - Judy Walton by TED-Ed:
>   https://www.youtube.com/watch?v=uihNc_tdGbk

The Constitution, the Articles, and Federalism: Crash Course US History #8 by CrashCourse:
>   https://www.youtube.com/watch?v=bO7FQsCcbD8

9. LEGENDS AND STORIES OF THE REVOLUTIONARY WAR

There are hundreds of well-researched, fact-based accounts of the battles and causes of the Revolutionary War. These accounts help modern Americans understand the hardships that their ancestors went through to create the American dream that many live today.

However, just as important as the fact-based accounts of the Revolutionary War are the legends, myths, and stories that have been passed down from generation to generation. Even stories of battlefield events do a lot to build the complete story of the Revolutionary War. While soldiers fought, hundreds of other people were working behind the scene to see America to victory. There is no way of telling if these myths have any seriousness to them, but they can enhance the story of the revolution. Some were not created or published until several years after the war ended.

Many of these stories were even passed around during wartime as stories to occupy the soldiers at night, so reading about them can put you in the mindset of a soldier in 1776. Imagine sitting between tents and horses after a long day of battle, a meager meal to fill you up, and a story to keep your mind off the next day's battle. You fall asleep dreaming of the strongest general in the world, a woman fighting in the war, and a covert officer hiding out in South Carolina.

9.1 MOLLY PITCHER

Figure 78. Molly Pitcher on the battlefield

According to legend, Molly Pitcher was a woman who participated in the Battle of Monmouth. It would be hundreds of years before women were officially allowed in the United States Army, but during the Revolutionary War, some women disguised themselves as men or found ways to participate on the battlefield.

Molly Pitcher, otherwise known as Molly Hays McCauly, was the wife of William Hays, an artilleryman. The story goes that she was with her husband, George Washington, and the Continental Army at their winter camp in Valley Forge. There she acted as a nurse to sick soldiers and assistant to her husband.

When the troops began the Battle of Monmouth, Molly was right in the field with them. She fetched water pitchers for overheated soldiers and guns, hence the nickname "pitcher." She also supposedly continued her nursing duties by lifting an injured soldier onto her back and carrying him off the field. But, perhaps Molly's most impressive feat was taking up her husband's gun when he fell in battle.

Other soldiers ordered Wiliam Hays and his gun to be removed from the field, but legend says Molly stepped right up and took control of the gun. She held her own against the British troops, despite heavy artillery, until the end of the battle.

Later, George Washington awarded Molly Pitcher the honor of "non-commissioned officer" for her bravery in the battle. The story of her courage was quickly passed around to all the soldiers of the Continental Army.

YouTube

Molly Pitcher, Folk Hero of the Revolutionary War by Biography:

    https://www.youtube.com/watch?v=ykOU714mVPg

The real woman behind the legend of Molly Pitcher by Fox News:

    https://www.youtube.com/watch?v=HSrlovPaUDg

9.2 GEORGE WASHINGTON AND THE SILVER DOLLAR

George Washington was a huge and strong man. He stood 6'2" tall and was incredibly strong. One legend that circulated amongst soldiers in the Continental Army at the time, and even persisted after Washington's death, was that, in a show of strength, the General threw a silver dollar coin across the Potomac River. Imagine Washington's massive arm winding up and launching that coin until no eyes could see it anymore. It sounds impressive. Imagine what it may have been like to witness it.

Sadly, the Potomac River is more than one mile wide, and while a silver dollar doesn't weigh much, not even Washington could have the strength to throw the coin a mile away. He did, however, throw a piece of slate over the Rappahannock River. Nevertheless, the descendants of George Washington continue to admire the strength of their ancestor.

The silver dollar was not minted until 1794, so that constitutes further evidence to debunk this legend.

9.3 SWAMP FOX

Figure 79. The Swamp Fox

Francis Marion, nicknamed the Swamp Fox by the British, was an American officer from South Carolina who managed to escape Charleston before the British captured South Carolina's capital city. His escape was a happy accident, as his true reason for leaving town was to mend a broken ankle he suffered during a dinner party a few weeks before the attack.

Marion, along with several other displaced Continental troops, hid out in the swamps of South Carolina. From the British perspective, Marion and his troops would attack seemingly out of nowhere, weaken their forces, and then disappear again.

The nickname Swamp Fox specifically refers to Marion's ability to go undetected in the South Carolina swamps. Foxes are traditionally tricksters, and so Marion was tricking and

Figure 80. South Carolina Swamps

evading the British who sought to capture him. They never succeeded, and so Marion continued to hide out in the swamps, occasionally resurfacing to make a surprise attack on the British forces.

While it is well documented that Marion hid in the South Carolina swamps and attacked the British, other reported feats of Marion were highly exaggerated. For example, he was no action hero as later books and movies would portray him. These tales attempt to romanticize Marion's wartime life. He was merely a resourceful fighter who helped make South Carolina as difficult for the British to hold as possible.

9.4 BETSY ROSS AND THE AMERICAN FLAG

Figure 81. Betsy Ross sewing the American flag

Most stories say that Betsy Ross was the seamstress who created the first American flag. In the legend, Ross was visited in her Pennsylvania home by George Washington, Robert Morris, and George Ross in 1776.

The three men asked her to review their sketch of the flag. That flag displayed 13 stars on a blue background and 13 red and white stripes. Ross reportedly accepted the assignment with a few changes, such as arranging the stars in a circle. The legend says that the flag flew above the battlefields and paints Ross as a kind of "mother" to the United States.

The flag was not officially adopted by the United States until 1777.

Figure 82. Francis Hopkinson

Betsy Ross's family supported this story, and her descendants verified it when the story was first published in Harper's New Monthly Magazine in 1873. Unfortunately, there is nothing more than family stories to actually verify the events. However, documentation does exist to prove Besty Ross's seamstress skills, as she is known to have sewn a flag for the Pennsylvania State Navy Board and Continental soldier's uniforms. Other accounts credit the flag's creation to Francis Hopkinson (Figure 82). Hopkinson also designed seals for the US Government.

9.5 THE BRITISH ARE COMING

Figure 83. The midnight ride of Paul Revere

According to popular legend, Paul Revere shouted from the back of his horse, "The British are coming, the British are coming!" as he rode through the Massachusetts countryside. This description paints a wonderful picture of a Revolutionary War hero, but it is likely just a legend.

At the time, the Sons of Liberty and other Patriots did not want the British to know they had intercepted their plans. Since the American militias were untrained and lacked power, they relied on the element of surprise.

Revere did take his midnight ride and successfully warned key revolutionary leaders about the coming of the British. However, it is more likely that he knocked on doors or left similarly lit lanterns to those hanging in the Old North Church in Boston.

9.6 MURDER OF JANE MCCREA

Figure 84. The capture of Jane McCrea

Jane McCrea was a beautiful woman who was engaged to David Jones, a Loyalist officer serving under British General John Burgoyne. As the British marched south from the Hudson Valley and evacuated Fort Ticonderoga and Fort Edward, Most colonists fled the area. However, McCrea refused to leave. Her future husband had written to her, wishing to see her if he were to pass through the Hudson Valley. According to legend, they were to be married at their secret meeting.

As McCrea waited for the troops and her love to arrive, two Native Americans arrived at Fort Edward. McCrea and another woman were captured by the Native Americans. These scouts were sent by the British to ensure no Continental forces awaited them. One of the women was returned to the British, but Sarah McCrea was murdered by the Native American scouts. She was found shot and scalped at Fort Edward. Her love was distraught, and so was the rest of America as word of her death spread like wildfire. The news even reached Great Britain. People were horrified that the woman had been killed. Her death did a lot to turn American opinion of the British and their allies. She was the victim of the highest-profile civilian killing of the entire war.

YouTube

Passage Minutes: The Story of Jane McCrea by Mountain Lake PBS:

> https://www.youtube.com/watch?v=V-OucUSQG7o

The Murder of Jane McCrae by Founders Club:

> https://www.youtube.com/watch?v=lBY3ZEBEk04

9.7 WHO WON THE MOST BATTLES OF THE REVOLUTIONARY WAR?

It is an easy assumption to make that America won the most battles of the Revolutionary War since the war ended in the American "victory." But, in reality, if we were to tally up all the wins, losses, and ties throughout the eight years of war, the British won more battles than the Continental Army.

Traditional war tactics, like standing shoulder to shoulder in an open field, defeated the Continental Army on most occasions, even in battles when the British were outnumbered. Meanwhile, American guerrilla warfare, which was highly uncommon then, was one of the only methods to win the Americans a few battles. General George Washington actually opposed guerrilla warfare, another fact that surprises most people. Guerrilla warfare was supported by other commanders like Nathanael Greene. Washington, however, wanted to meet and beat the British in a grand, European-style battle. He finally got that chance at the Battle of Yorktown.

The two sides were using many of the same resources, like muskets and cannons, to fight each other, so neither side had an advantage in technology.

10. CONCLUSION

Figure 85. George Washington elected 1st president

In the wake of the Revolutionary War, General George Washington was elected the first President of the United States. He served from 1789 to 1797. Upon his resignation from office, Washington advised his successors to avoid political parties, hoping that by leaving office, he would help citizens understand that the president was different than a king. The president would not rule forever.

Of course, many of Washington's pieces of advice were not heeded. The second President of the United States, John Adams, ruled the country for one term, and as political parties organized, so did the tension in the country.

The United States would not fight another major war on its soil until 1861. The Civil War from 1861 to 1865 would see the secession of several Southern States to form the Confederacy.

These Southern States seceded for many reasons, including the issue of slavery, state's rights, and other grievances with the 16th President of the United States, Abraham Lincoln.

Stay tuned for the next exciting installment of Awesome Battles for Kids when we march onto the battlefield with the Union and Confederate soldiers to witness the outcome of one of America's bloodiest wars, The Civil War.

YouTube

Passage Minutes: The Story of Jane McCrea by Mountain Lake PBS:

https://www.youtube.com/watch?v=V-OucUSQG7o

The Murder of Jane McCrae by Founders Club:

https://www.youtube.com/watch?v=lBY3ZEBEko4

11. ABOUT THE AUTHOR

Ryan Rhoderick is a seasoned writer dedicated to bringing history to life for readers, especially children. Specializing in military history, he has written a series of captivating books that delve into the awesome world of battles, strategies, and heroic feats. Through rich storytelling and exhaustive research, Ryan Rhoderick aims to encourage a passion for learning and an appreciation for the triumphs and challenges faced by soldiers and leaders throughout history. Via his books, Awesome Battles for Kids, he inspires and educates, making history an exhilarating adventure for young minds.

To find out about upcoming books, join our thriving Facebook Community at: bit.ly/49pIE7o

If you enjoyed this book, you are encouraged to leave a review on the book's page on Amazon.com

Printed in the USA
CPSIA information can be obtained
at www.ICGtesting.com
LVHW021002030424
776292LV00016B/143